Poetry, Prose and Art in the American Social Gospel Movement 1880-1910

POETRY, PROSE AND ART IN THE AMERICAN SOCIAL GOSPEL MOVEMENT 1880-1910

John C. Waldmeir

Texts and Studies in the Social Gospel
Volume 4

The Edwin Mellen Press
Lewiston•Queenston•Lampeter

Library of Congress Cataloging-in-Publication Data

Waldmeir, John Christian, 1959-
Poetry, prose and art in the American social gospel movement, 1880-1910 / by John C. Waldmeir.
p. cm. -- (Text & studies in the social gospel ; v. 4)
Includes bibliographical references and index.
ISBN-0-7734-7261-4
1. Social gospel--History--19th century. 2. Socialism, Christian--North America--History--19th century. 3. North America--Church history--19th century. 4. Social gospel--History--20th century. 5. Socialism, Christian--North America--History--20th century. 6. North America--Church history--20th century. I. Title. II. Texts and studies in the social gospel ; v. 4.

BT738 .W287 2002
277.3'08--dc21

2001044720

This is volume 4 in the continuing series
Texts and Studies in the Social Gospel
Volume 4 ISBN 0-7734-7261-4
TSSG Series ISBN 0-7734-8728-X

A CIP catalog record for this book is available from the British Library.

The Edwin Mellen Press
Box 450
Lewiston, New York
USA 14092-0450

The Edwin Mellen Press
Box 67
Queenston, Ontario
CANADA L0S 1L0

The Edwin Mellen Press, Ltd.
Lampeter, Ceredigion, Wales
UNITED KINGDOM SA48 8LT

Printed in the United States of America

"To seek a new approach and a new answer to the problems of the human condition is to criticize the old. And to find or reaffirm the most ancient of answers, love and individual responsibility, is to make that criticism explicit—to make it at once an accusation, a challenge, and a demand for reform."

Joseph J. Waldmeir
"Quest Without Faith"

FOR MICHAEL AND HELEN PETRISKO
WHO MADE QUESTIONS AND ANSWERS FROM THE
EARLY TWENTIETH CENTURY COME ALIVE

TABLE OF CONTENTS

ILLUSTRATIONS
ix

PREFACE
xi

FOREWORD
xiii

ACKNOWLEDGMENT
xv

INTRODUCTION
1
"The Voice of God in the Story":
Ambiguity and the Social Christian Imagination

CHAPTER ONE
19
"Not Other, More":
Social Christianity and the Rhetoric of Wholeness

CHAPTER TWO
37
Filling in the Blanks
Absence and Presence in the Works of Charles Sheldon

CHAPTER THREE
55
Social Christianity and the Problem of the West

CHAPTER FOUR
79
Christian Socialism and God's Plot

CHAPTER FIVE
99
The Person in Social Christian Literature

CONCLUSION
115
A New Sacredness

SOURCES
123

INDEX
131

ILLUSTRATIONS

FIG. 1 Frank Beard
As Conscience Paints Him
From *Fifty Great Cartoons* (Chicago: The Ram's Horn Press, 1899)

FIG. 2 Frank Beard
His Real Self
From *Fifty Great Cartoons* (Chicago: The Ram's Horn Press, 1899)

FIG. 3 Olof Grafström, *View of Portland, Oregon* (1890)
The Fine Arts Museums of San Francisco, Museum Collection

FIG. 4 Joseph Hitchens *Admission of Colorado to the Union* or
Jerome Chaffee Introduces Miss Columbia to Miss Colorado (1884)
Colorado Historical Society, Denver.

FIG. 5 George Harvey, *View of Burlington* (1892)
Burlington Public Library, Burlington, IA

FIG. 6 *North Dakota Magazine* 1 (May, 1906)

FIG. 7 Hebjorn Gausta, *The Lay Preacher* (1884)
Vesterheim, Norwegian-American Museum, Decorah, IA

FIG 8 J. Laurie Wallace
William Jennings Bryan (1902)
Nebraska State Historical Society, Lincoln

PREFACE

Since the publication of Arthur Schlesinger, Sr.'s essay, "A Critical Period in American Religion, 1875-1900," the social gospel has emerged as a topic of ongoing historical fascination. In the decades since Schlesinger's essay first appeared in the 1930s, the topic has been examined from a variety of perspectives through numerous critical essays and monographs. At the same time, social gospel scholarship has been characterized by a tendency to focus exclusively on the movement's place within the history of American Protestantism. These studies have largely cast the social gospel as a movement dominated by elite cadres of church leaders, drawn from various centers of influence and power from what has come to be known as "the Protestant establishment."

This book by John Waldmeir suggests a fresh alternative for understanding the social gospel's influence in America. What makes this study unique is that Waldmeir doesn't simply rehash earlier scholarly discourses on the social gospel, seeing the movement only from the institutional confines of late 19th century Protestant Christianity. He demonstrates how the intellectual and theological currents that scholars would later call, "the social gospel" played a major role in shaping the ideological worldview of late nineteenth-century American culture. Whether through the rhetoric of religious and Progressive-Era leaders, the writings of popular fiction or the visual imagery of contemporary art, Waldmeir demonstrates how social gospel ideals captivated the popular imagination of an emerging middle-class audience. He asserts that the social gospel was more than the theological stances taken by professional theologians and church leaders; it was a psychological orientation that reflected how many Americans of that era viewed the relationship of the individual to their larger social environment.

Scholars who read this volume will not only find Waldmeir's interpretation of the social gospel thought provoking, they will discover that his conclusions challenge future researchers to broaden their understanding of the social gospel's influence upon the contours of American religious and cultural history. This book makes readers think in new ways about how one defines "the social gospel."

Christopher H. Evans
Associate Professor of Church History
Colgate Rochester Crozer Divinity School
May, 2001

Foreword

The large late nineteenth and early twentieth-century movement called social Christianity has come to be identified with its most famous component, the Social Gospel, and so the title of this book. People searching computer data bases for information about the theologians, writers, artists and ideas discussed here are likely to enter the phrase *social gospel* in their queries, and in these days of instantaneous response, it is important to have references to your work "on the screen" quickly if you want it read.

In the course of writing a forward to what this work contains, it might be helpful if I refer first to what it does not include. Readers will not find here one more attempt to sort the diverse social Christian or Social Gospel movement into categories traditionally labeled "liberal," "conservative," and "middle of the road," or "left," "right," and "center." Such sorting has preoccupied many who have written about this movement, and although it has produced worthwhile results, one of my claims is that, in the end, the categories fail to contain the available material. Perhaps another way of making the same point would be to say that, once students of the movement consider the remarkable variety of genres represented by social Christianity, fresh ways of understanding the movement present themselves. As my title suggests, this study proposes that the arts are more important to the movement and its identity than previously thought.

If *Poetry, Prose and Art in the Social Gospel Movement* does not consciously try to organize its sources according to a pre-conceived set of traditional categories, neither does it eschew those categories in favor of a new set of terms introduced by contemporary critical theory. A number of critical approaches inform this work, most notably those attempts at re-reading the past that together comprise a "new" historicism. In this work I deliberately have avoided the now common practice of rehearsing one or two recent theoretical approaches or methods in the early chapters only to then "apply" them in subsequent ones. I am not naïve enough to think I can write about social Christian "texts" without some attention to the hermeneutic that controls my inquiry. I do believe, however, that at this juncture in the critical enterprise readers do not need to hear at length from authors about the theorist who has shaped their thinking most profoundly. Too often such homage further blunts what the eminent scholar of Religion and Literature, Anthony C. Yu, calls the "predictable" and "rather dull picture of the literary world" advanced in so much criticism today.

Although it is not fashionable, it certainly is true that I have tried to let my sources determine my approach. In selecting them I have omitted a great deal, but my citations and bibliography should enable readers to pursue their interests and either expand upon or challenge my conclusions. The ideals represented by the Social Gospel movement need to be rediscovered by every generation, especially now in these early days of the twenty-first century when the world is with us in terror and fear. I hope this book stimulates an interest in the movement, discussion of its principles, and a willingness to think and act charitably toward its goals.

ACKNOWLEDGMENT

Chapter three, "Social Christianity and the Problem of the West," was written with the help of a grant given by National Endowment for the Humanities and distributed through the North Dakota Humanities Council.

INTRODUCTION

"THE VOICE OF GOD IN THE STORY": AMBIGUITY AND THE SOCIAL CHRISTIAN IMAGINATION

> "In the parable of the Prodigal Son, or of the Good Samaritan, we do not demand that the events that are described shall have actually occurred, before we can hear the voice of God in the story. . . .
>
> William Newton Clarke, *Sixty Years with the Bible* (1909)

A wealth of social Christian novels, poetry, and visual images came together during the late nineteenth and early twentieth-centuries to help Americans imagine new roles for God in a society that had acquired a host of identities. Treated increasingly as "immanent" within this world instead of "other" than it, God came to life in such imaginative works, and through the elements of creative expression—setting, scene, plot, character, tone, style, meter, metaphor, etc. – social Christian writers, artists, ministers, theologians, and others demonstrated ways that experience in the nineteenth-century could provide believers with meaningful images of the divine.

These imaginative works have been sorted in various ways and frequently interpreted as "reflections" of the age and environment that inspired them. Seldom, however, have they been valued as literature or, perhaps more reasonably, as serious examples of religious rhetoric from this period. Rarely, in fact, have students of social Christianity valued imaginative expressions of its beliefs as interesting, let alone provocative.[1] The sheer weight of social Christian material makes this omission suspect. With approximately 1300 novels attributed to the topic, social Christian literature constitutes a potent influence upon the culture and society it depicts.[2] Together these texts help to fashion a system of knowledge, a view of reality.[3]

---

[1] John P. Ferre's 1988 book about best-selling novels is typical of most studies that treat imaginative social Christian literature form the late nineteenth and early twentieth-centuries. According to Ferre, novels like Sheldon's *In His Steps*, Gordon's *Black Rock*, and Wright's *The Calling of Dan Matthews* all "reveal the dominant religious belief system of the American middle class" during this period. Their value to students of American social Christianity, Ferre argues, is that they "illustrate the changes in commerce, technology, and law at the dawn of the twentieth century" and "indicate moral responses to the changes that the country was undergoing at the time." Ferre of course is correct, but his argument falls short of what is needed to explain why novels like these are important. These books not only "reveal" belief systems, "illustrate" social changes, and "indicate" moral responses, they shape all three. Readers need not accept the premise of much contemporary ideological criticism, which holds that people write fiction for political reasons, to recognize that such books do more than mirror their age. John P. Ferre, *A Social Gospel for the Millions, The Religious Bestsellers of Charles Sheldon, Charles Gordon, and Harold Bell Wright* (Bowling Green, OH: Bowling Green State U. Press, 1988): 14.

[2] For a thorough study of this extensive genre, see Robert Glenn Wright, *The Social Christian Novel* (Westport, CT: Greenwood Press, 1989).

[3] Sociologists like George Thomas call systems or theories like this one "ontologies" because they help coordinate the world we depict with the meanings we generate when we interpret that world. One "orients oneself and one's actions to institutional rules," writes Thomas, "not only in the interest of 'social order' but also in the interest of meaning." Such "rules" create a framework that both enforces hegemony and explains why one form of organization is better than another. For example, as another sociologist, Max Weber, claimed, the creation of "a Protestant *ethic*" did indeed compel believers to act in rational ways; however, argues Thomas, the formation of "a Protestant *ontology* defined a reality in which rational activity and organization . . . made sense and came to be morally binding." George M. Thomas, *Revivalism and Cultural Change, Christianity, Nation Building, and the Market in the Nineteenth-Century United States*. (Chicago: U. of Chicago Press, 1989), 14-15, 22-23.

By neglecting this body of literature students of the movement have tended to forget the extent to which imaginative expressions define a social Christian witness. Perhaps the only figure more impressive than the number of novels associated with the movement is the volume sold. As John P. Ferre has shown, social Christian novels alone carried the message of the movement to more than ten million readers. When readers consider genre other than the novel, that number grows considerably. Not only do social Christian magazines like *The Dawn* and *The Kingdom*, for example, publish poets and short story authors, they also promote visual artists whose paintings and photographs become part of the social Christian worldview. Imaginative expressions of all kinds become vehicles for a social Christian message, and often that creativity appears in unexpected places, like art reviews by the great social Christian theologian, Walter Rauschenbusch, or novels by its most prominent minister, Washington Gladden.

The wealth and diversity of materials raises an obvious and, for students of social Christianity, a persistent question: what belongs to this movement? In their respective studies of the period and its documents, Robert Glenn Wright and Henry F. May, for example, both spend a great deal of time sorting the vast literature. Wright reads virtually every available novel and places each one into a category: (a) "Fictional expressions of vague, abstract, transcendental Christian humanism"; (b) "Social gospel tracts"; (c) "Works that concentrate on theoretical political radicalism based on Christian ethics"; (d)"Socially and theologically conservative novels that stress traditional forms of charity." May's history of *Protestant Churches and Industrial America* sifts the religious writings into three broad areas: "Conservative Social Christianity," "Progressive Social Christianity (The Social Gospel)," and "Radical Social Christianity."[4] May's approach also structures the presentation of material in two additional sourcebooks, Paul Boase's *The Rhetoric of Christian Socialism* and the collection compiled by C.

Howard Hopkins and Ronald White, *The Social Gospel, Religion and Reform in a Changing America.*[5]

All of these works are valuable, and the categories they isolate are extremely useful. Their common approach, however, does not address an observation Boase himself makes in the opening pages of his introduction. After noting that *The Christian Century* pronounced the Social Gospel dead in 1962, Boase points out that "Social concern born of religion has had its obituary read before, only to spring back to life, usually modified, often with new brilliance."[6] Though they are useful, the distinctions between "conservative, progressive, and liberal" or "left, center, and right" do not give readers the means to understand why a social Christianity endures, especially during a century when almost all motives to social or cultural change are secular.

The answer may have less to do with the message and more to do with its medium. The number of novels, poems, and pictures associated with the movement suggests that creativity is essential to its value; what makes rich and compelling social Christian beliefs in the salvation of whole communities or the creation of God's kingdom on earth are the ways numerous advocates express their convictions. Not only do novelists, poets, and painters from the movement depend upon the figurative use of language to make their points, so do theologians, ministers, and social commentators. Together, the images they employ and the metaphors they produce constitute a creative style that helps to keep social Christianity alive throughout the twentieth century. Critics and interested readers can observe a debt to this style in the rhetoric of national civil rights movements and the premises of numerous theologies of liberation. The

---

[4] Wright, *The Social Christian Novel*, especially page 111; Henry F. May *Protestant Churches and Industrial America* (New York: Octagon Books, 1949, 1977).

[5] Paul H. Boase, ed. *The Rhetoric of Christian Socialism* (New York: Random House, 1969); C. Howard Hopkins and Ronald C. White, eds. *The Social Gospel: Religion and Reform in a Changing America* (Philadelphia: Temple U. Press, 1976).

[6] Boase, *The Rhetoric of Christian Socialism*, 4.

fruits of creativity, and the imagination that nurtures its roots, have prevented a final social Christian obituary from being written.

Such imagination has not, however, necessarily made this movement more single-minded or well-focused. Indeed, when taken seriously, the social Christian imagination tends to disturb the otherwise comfortable arrangement of its practitioners into those traditional groups of "left," "right," and "center." Moreover, that imagination also introduces an element of ambiguity into our interpretations of texts that long have defined its methods and meanings. Social Christianity demonstrates fully what Garrett Green calls the "systematic ambiguity" of the religious imagination.[7] Its function prevents students of American culture from dismissing the late nineteenth and early twentieth-century manifestation of the movement as merely a "period piece," abandoned with the onset of a century of world war and civil unrest. Neither uniform nor consistent, the social Christian proclamation nevertheless has been more than just an ideal left buried during the very season when we needed most to hear it.

An interesting place to begin a recovery of this creative style and its imaginative source is with a figure from the era who William Hutchison labels an "outstanding systematizer," Biblical scholar William Newton Clarke.[8] A Baptist theologian at Hamilton (Colgate) Theological Seminary, Clarke is intriguing because he finds ways to fashion his "system" that are not very "systematic" at all. "My life had given me my method with the Bible," he wrote in 1912. To questions about the "revolution" in Biblical criticism "to which my generation was born," Clarke answered: "the best witness [to faith] is experience." And although his method sometimes led Clarke to claim naively that, when faced with

---

[7] Garrett Green, *Imagining God, Theology and the Religious Imagination*. Grand Rapids: Wm. B. Eerdman's, 1989: 62. Green's excellent analysis argues that the imagination helps us to "pattern life" and that the religious imagination in particular offers us a pattern "of 'what the world is like' in its broadest and deepest sense."

[8] William R. Hutchison, The Modernist Impulse in American Protestantism (New York: Oxford U. Press, 1976), 117.

difficult questions, he "could read the [Bible] and get [his] information," it also motivated him to reflect in sophisticated ways upon "a more interior and spiritual idea of evidence of the present God." In Clarke's so-called system, "Theology should be a result of exegesis, but as a second fruit, not a first." To be understood fully, the "testimonies to divine reality" that appear in Scripture "must pass into theology through life."[9]

Clarke describes the theological concept of a God who is "immanent" within all creation, but he does so through references to his own experiences. Furthermore, when he joins these experiences together, he discovers that they comprise the outlines of a story, "an autobiography" that reveals to Clarke a plot. "By a sure and unceasing guidance," he writes, "I have been brought along the way to the present goal." The goal is to explicate a "text" that contains both Biblical and personal narratives for, as Clarke insists, "my whole life had been leading me toward . . .a theologian's task." In the end it is as a theologian that he confesses to his readers: "If I could tell the story in any person but the first I should do so, but I cannot."[10] Neither "the large work of the Nineteenth Century upon the Bible" nor the admission that he has "passed through the revolution" of higher Biblical criticism provides Clarke with the exegetical resources to create his system. He needs the drama of personal experience.

With the help of such experience Clarke is able to interpret texts differently than was possible under "the old attitude toward the Bible."[11] "God is in the story" now, writes Clarke, as immanent and alive as any author who writes his own narrative, and this "location" for God motivates Clarke to introduce an appropriate literary terminology. Although the Bible remains "sacred," it also becomes "an ancient book," indeed a "collection of books" valued for their

---

[9] William Newton Clarke, *Sixty Years with the Bible, A Record of Experience* (New York: Charles Scribner's Sons, 1912), 5-6, 193-207.

[10] *Ibid.*, 8-9

[11] *Ibid.*, 4-5.

"'worth and beauty.'"[12] When Clarke "tells the story" of how his Biblical exegesis evolved over a sixty-year period, he does so "in the single character of a student, lover, and user of the Bible." Inclined to treat the text as a work of the imagination, Clarke pays attention to its "similes" and "style" and repeatedly uses metaphors to describe his theological approach.[13] At one point he says that the story acts like "timbers" for "the frame of [his] system"; at another that it serves as the "warp and woof" for God's message. For Clarke, the God who resides in the Gospel stories is "a character" who reveals himself through poetic images, his message "shines by his own light," and its "revelation is not a lightening flash: it is rather like the dawn, brightening into the full day."[14]

Such poetic imagery is not necessarily the product of systematic thinking. It is, however, consistent with Clarke's autobiographical and experiential approach to his subject matter. That fact alters Hutchison's characterization of Clarke and challenges the polarity he tries to establish between the Biblical scholar's "systematization" and the broad appeal of a "champion popularizer" from the same time like Lyman Abbot.[15] Furthermore, as imagination and the creative use of language by a range of social Christian writers disrupts one polarity in Hutchison, it also threatens a second. In his now classic definition of one branch of the larger social Christian movement, the Social Gospel, Hutchison writes that the term "has sometimes been lifted out of its late-nineteenth-century context and made the generic equivalent of 'religious social reform.'" This approach, argues Hutchison, permits "an enormous number of theological conservatives, as well as many more liberals [to] be called proponents or prophets of the Social Gospel." Such an effort to define the term so broadly only "muddies the waters considerably" because, he points out, virtually every nineteenth-century religious denomination promoted some form of social reform, from antislavery

---

[12] *Ibid.*, 236, 255-256.

[13] *Ibid.*, 156, 176.

[14] *Ibid.*, 199,221.

movements to urban missions to calls for temperance. Because such "crusades" were common, Hutchison maintains that:

> It was something else again to argue, as Social Gospelers did, that social salvation precedes individual salvation both temporally and in importance. Even to give social reform an equal, nonderivative status was a move quite distinct in theory. . . . It was this theoretical elevation of social salvation, therefore, that made the Social Gospel a distinctive movement.[16]

There are two crucial features to Hutchison's definition. In the first, Hutchison focuses attention on the interplay between individual and social salvation; in the second, he argues that the way social Christians addressed that interplay was through a type of discourse called "theoretical." These two points certainly are related, but not necessarily the way Hutchison maintains. It is correct to point out that the central distinction in social Christianity, perhaps especially in the Social Gospel, is between the individual and society. The curious fact, however, is not that the two remain separate, like two more poles around which the movement organizes itself. On the contrary, the remarkable feature is that social Christian discussions of individuality almost always raise social issues while references to society repeatedly occasion the rhetoric of individual life and salvation. Hutchison can assert that, in the Social Gospel at least, social salvation precedes the saving of individual lives. The more striking claim, though, is that within this wide range of ministers, theologians, social scientists, novelists, lawyers, and poets, few seem inclined to articulate a notion of social salvation without reference to certain patterns associated with individual life.[17]

It is a striking claim and it raises Hutchison's second point. The relationship between the individual and society in social Christian writing does

---

[15] Hutchison, *The Modernist Impulse*, 116-17.

[16] Hutchison, *The Modernist Impulse in American Protestantism*, 165.

[17] An exception to this point appears in writings from the branch of social Christianity typically referred to as "Christian Socialism." For a full discussion of this exception see Chapter 4 below.

require a special discourse, and insofar as that discourse is theological it is also theoretical. But again such theory is only part of what is involved when social Christians discuss individual and social lives. Nothing less than an act of imagination allows these writers to overcome the distinction the movement posits between the one and the many. The logic behind the theory is often theological, but in the broadest sense it also is poetic, a way of thinking that relies upon the transformative power of language to denote the world and at the same time to recreate it through multiple and often contradictory connotations.

These recurring contradictions are what prompt Martin Marty to describe American religion between 1893 and 1919 with a literary term, calling it an age of "irony." Marty narrates a story of all modern American religion during these years that emphasizes the disjunctions between intentions and outcomes. Social Christian writers and ministers from the late nineteenth and early twentieth centuries created for their audiences a world view that permitted if not encouraged such irony. When social Christians sought "wholeness" their words suggested division; when they spoke of God's presence they noted his absence; when they imagined a new land west of the Mississippi they steeped it in images from ancient history.

Within social Christianity it is interesting to try and trace the origins of this irony. One place to begin would be with the origins of the term that Hutchison defines so incisively, the Social Gospel.[18] According to several historians, including Marty, Howard Hopkins, and Ronald White, the term "Social

---

[18] Even the act of bringing these the two words together seems to promote irony. According to Thomas Chases's work on the English religious lexis, the terms "social" and "gospel" belong to different lexical fields. "Gospel" of course is a part of the lexicon of terms we use to talk about "Belief, Doctrine, and Spirituality" while the term "social" implies a more tangible realm of "Worship, Ritual, and Practice." This juxtaposition of references to tangible and intangible realities occurs again in the phrase that appears at the center of the entire social Christian movement, the "Kingdom of God." In the history of religious discourse in English, "Kingdom" has been associated with material artifacts and "God" has been the subject of faith and the object of creedal statements. Thomas Chase, *The English Religious Lexis* (Lewiston: Edwin Mellen Press, 1988).

Gospel" first was used in 1886 by a Congregational minister in Dubuque, Iowa named Charles O. Brown, who intended (ironically) to give it a pejorative meaning. As all three scholars have pointed out, Brown's book, *Talks on the Labor Troubles*, associated the term disapprovingly with the writings of Henry George, especially *Progress and Poverty.* Because of George's aim to promote an "entire change in the relation of capital to labor," Reverend Brown labeled the book "extreme," "revolutionary," and "utterly unreasonable," complaining that its ideas, which constituted a new "social gospel," were "affecting the views of millions," especially those in "laborer's cottages" and in "laboring men's clubs."[19]

It is ironic indeed that the Social Gospel influenced "laborers" far less than it did the middle class Americans who read Brown's book. But if Brown was wrong to associate the phrase with wholesale change among working class Americans, he was correct to describe its impact as culturally pervasive. In order to appreciate this level of irony, however, readers need to return to the original *Talks* and examine them more closely, because although Hopkins, White, and Marty all note the references to *Progress and Poverty* in Brown, there is a second citation that perhaps is even more significant.

According to Brown, the Social Gospel shares ideas with *Progress and Poverty* but owes its influence to another text. "No book of the present century," writes Brown, "except *Uncle Tom's Cabin*" can illustrate the way George's ideas have changed society. We can adjust the economic or political matrices typically labeled "wealthy, middle, lower classes," or "conservative, progressive, radical" but, suggests Brown, unless we broaden our configuration to include the contributions of imaginative expression, we neglect the most significant resource for change that is available within the tradition. Thus Brown insists that, if we

[19] Charles O. Brown, *Talks on the Labor Troubles* (Chicago: F.H. Revel, 1886), 9-10. White and Hopkins refer to Brown as the one who "first used" the phrase, and Marty corroborates their account. See White and Hopkins, *The Social Gospel, Religion and Reform in a Changing America*, 167 n. 13; Marty, *The Irony of It All*, 362, n. 14:10.

want to understand the true importance of ideas associated with the Social Gospel, "it may be well for us to remember the influence that *Uncle Tom's Cabin* exerted in the abolition of slavery." Throughout *Talks on the Labor Troubles* Brown is sensitive to the role of imaginative literature and the kind of literary symbolism that can inflame a rhetoric of social change. Furthermore, he points out that the rhetorical value of such literature and symbolism is not restricted to works of high or low culture. To the bad poetry of a Chicago labor sheet and the popular lyrics of "My Country 'tis of Thee," Brown adds references to Milton, Matthew Arnold, Mazzini, and Defoe.

As a Congregationalist minister to a rather typical midwestern parish, Brown represents the attitudes of numerous clergy from the period. In fact, three years after they read *Talks on the Labor Troubles*, Brown's congregation heard from a number of preachers during a "semi-centennial celebration" that brought to Dubuque former pastors, speakers, and other guests. In their homilies and reflections these ministers all focused their attention on the relation between "an assimilation to God" attempted by individuals and a social order fashioned around belief in the "oneness among men."[20] During this celebration, Brown describes the most difficult obstacle that exists for those who want to describe accurately the relationship between individuals and the Church, parishioners and their parish. "The life of [that relationship] can never be written," asserts Brown. "The laughter and tears, the songs of praise, the shouts of triumph, the humiliations of defeat, the revivals of religion, the ingatherings, the removals and the deaths – ah! Volumes are hidden here which will never be written on earth."[21]

The preachers at Dubuque's First Congregational Church who nevertheless try in 1889 to respond to this challenge do not turn to systematic theology for their models. Instead they use their imaginations. An outstanding

[20] C.O. Brown, ed., *Semi Centennial Celebration of the First Congregational Church of Dubuque, Iowa, May 12th and 13th, 1889* (Dubuque, First Congregational Church, 1889), 32.
[21] *Ibid.*, 75.

example is J.S. Bingham, who symbolizes the social Christian nation that is destined to emerge when the Social Gospel is able to "permeate and fuse the masses into one righteous brotherhood." He writes of "Columbia, the peerless queen," who

> steps out upon that marvelous pedestal of the attained ideal of a Christian nation, upon which is sculptured in characters of dazzling brightness, Faith, Hope and Charity, and stands robed in the red, white and blue of national integrity, and each representing a sovereign State, with its free schools, and colleges and churches, and rapidly increasing intelligent millions . . . [and] presents to the astonished world the symbol of the first fruits of Christianity's attained ideal in a sheaf of ripened grain, bound by an indissoluble band upon which is inscribed, "The United States of America, the sample sheaf of a redeemed world. . . ."[22]

Bingham's goddess exhibits the imagination and irony that defines so much social Christian expression. An eighteenth-century emblem of the emerging nation, Columbia here represents a future that stretches before Bingham into the twentieth. Symbol of immanence within humanity, Bingham's Columbia is elevated upon a pedestal above her subjects. The image of an ideal social unity, she is associated with individual figures and items: Faith, Hope and Charity, separate sovereign States, intelligent millions, grain within a sheaf. Symbolic expression of a relationship that, according to Brown, cannot be written, Columbia nevertheless explains herself in words.

Lyman Abbott opened his 1896 book *Christianity and Social Problems* with the words "Christ's mission was twofold – individual and social. . . ."[23] He closed it with the claim that

> "the problem of our American commonwealth is to teach men the meaning of words which run so glibly from our tongues, -- justice and liberty; to teach what are the laws under which men and women should live; to sweep away the cant that obscures the word

---

[22] *Ibid.*, 32-33.

[23] Lyman Abbott, *Christianity and Social Problems* (Boston: Houghton Mifflin, 1896), iii.

> "brotherhood," and to give it a clear and definite meaning, not by words chiefly, but by our lives and our national identity.[24]

Like Bingham's image of Columbia, Abbott's commonwealth is a sheaf of words that, ironically, are obscured by other words and finally understood only by actions that transcend words altogether. Between the conviction that Christ's mission was twofold and the depiction of a commonwealth that also is double in its dependence upon and independence of words lies Abbott's discussion of Biblical "narrative," his references to individual growth as a metaphor for social development, his description of Christ's words as "pictures," his allusions to Whittier's "Eternal Goddess" and Hawthorne's *Scarlet Letter.* Through these references Abbott does not simply polish his argument, he actually grounds his claims in the style, content, and structure of imaginative expression. In this way the rationale that shapes his thinking depends upon something like the logic of poetry.

Social Christians who ascribe religious meanings both to individual lives and social organizations do more than reflect their age. They dramatize its problems and possibilities and, in so doing, indirectly advance many of its ironic tensions. Consider the image that appears on the cover of this study. Drawn by Frank Beard, a prolific "cartoonist" who published many works in the social Christian magazine, *The Ram's Horn*, it depicts several themes that arise with varying degrees of emphasis throughout the movement. The social Christian concern with poverty is apparent in the action that takes place beneath the hovering angel and child. This poverty is a consequence of the setting, which appears to be both urban and industrial, two realms that social Christians sought to redeem. The landscape is confusing with its mix of unkempt streets, smoke stacks, and distant steeples, and both the melee below and the battered child above indicate that the confusion has led to violence. The prominence of the "saloon,"

---

[24] *Ibid.*, 368-69.

its relation to fighting in the street, and the distress of the woman who stands apart from the crowd link the picture to yet another social Christian theme, "temperance."

Although all of these topics are consistent with social Christian concerns, the messages conveyed by Beard's drawing are far more ambiguous. Given that all forms of social Christianity sought to diminish evil and promote changes within the social fabric of American life, viewers of this image should question why the "rescue" it depicts leaves behind such a troubled world. Why doesn't God's angel bring order to the streets and calm the violence? More specifically, why does God choose to gather the boy in death instead of taking a more active role in reforming the social turmoil that, as the lengthy caption suggests, leads to his end?[25] Where is the manifestation of that symbol that is so prominent within social Christian theology, the Kingdom of God?

Such questions are not ideologically neutral. In fact, they imply the sort of skepticism that is typical of recent cultural studies dedicated to this era of American life. Most of these studies recognize little if any critical perspective in the artistic, social, and political movements that dominate the late nineteenth and early twentieth centuries. Neither the dramatic improvement in photographic arts nor the creation of its literary counterpart, realism; neither the social dynamics of that novel enterprise called "shopping" nor the political agenda of a "Progressive" platform—nothing satisfies the demands of most contemporary critics who long to discover a critical idiom that transcends the hegemony of dominant middle class

---

[25] The full caption reads: "Wherever the tide of human life flows very deeply and swiftly, there shipwreck is most frequent and we place Rescue Missions at these points. But do we ever think of there being rescue missions in the skies? Could we scan the far battlements of heaven we might, perhaps, see them lined with hosts of angels watching and waiting to descend to the rescue of some tender child whom it were better to snatch away to scenes of glory, than to leave in an atmosphere that reeks with moral contagion. It was such a scene as appears [here] that Isaiah saw when he wrote `He shall gather the lambs with his arm and shall carry them in his bosom.'" *Fifty Great Cartoons* (Chicago, The Ram's Horn Press, 1899), unpaginated.

rhetoric and attitudes. In the minds of many critics, social Christianity, with its range of contradictory theologies and concerns, provides no serious alternative.

But its limitations are no more restrictive than those that emerge from the theories and practices of other religious movements, all of which struggle to negotiate the "natural and supernatural," "God and man," the "sacred and profane." Beard's image illustrates elements of one particular moment in this continuous process of negotiation. What is interesting for purposes of this study is the position Beard allots to "art" in his depiction. The angel who carries away the child is not simply different from this environment because he is "heavenly," he is distinct because he is beautiful, a work of classical art in an otherwise artless scene. The angel does not simply rescue him from "moral contagion," he carries him away to "scenes of glory." Just as the temperance theme gains prominence because the saloon appears in a place that is central to the composition of the work, the angel's individual beauty becomes significant because Beard draws it against this particular social backdrop.

This interaction between the world of the city and the realm of God takes viewers directly to one of the most important contributions social Christianity makes to "modern" American theology: the belief that Christians can introduce and preserve ultimate meaning and value in life through the risks they take as creatures of history. God's own "creativeness" in this process, as Eugene Lyman of Union Theological Seminary contended in 1918, is an "ever present fact and a vital experience;" it demands, argued Henry Churchill King in 1907, nothing less than a "frank acceptance of the doctrine of eternal creation."[26] This enduring need for divine creativity alerted many social Christians to the corresponding value of

---

[26] Eugene Lyman, *The God of the New Age* (Boston: Pilgrim, 1918), 13. Quoted in William McGuire King, "'History as Revelation' in the Theology of the Social Gospel," *Harvard Theological Review* 76 (1983): 123. Henry Churchill King, Theology and the Social Consciousness (New York: Macmillan, 1907), 215. Quoted in King, "'History as Revelation' in the Theology of the Social Gospel," 123.

human creation. As a result, social Christian art, novels, poetry, and even theology emphasized the role of God in the otherwise "human" process of living, thinking, and working creatively. As a more recent scholar, William McGuire King, points out, the first and second generation of theologians who wrote in the social Christian tradition learned that "religious values were not . . . discoverable *a priori*"; rather, they found that such value "had to be generated through human decision and action." In this way the "world of human interaction and social struggle" was "viewed as the place where religious meaning and value were generated and conserved."[27]

As King reads social Christian theology from the period, he finds that its emphasis upon the contingencies of human action tend to produce in this line of inquiry "an intellectual paradox." Indeed, as he demonstrates, a series of paradoxes arise from the twin convictions of social Christian theologians who recognized "the genuine indeterminacy of historical events" and at the same time "stressed the social character and contingency of God's own being."[28] Perhaps no one summarizes this paradoxical situation better that Josiah Strong who, in 1886, turns to metaphor and states simply: "God has two hands." With this figure of speech, which appears in *Our Country*, a popular tract for the American Missionary Association that sold 175,000 copies, Strong denotes a sacred figure who is able to help us establish his Kingdom. But (ironically) his image signifies even more, for in a text like *Our Country*, one that repeatedly introduces objective "facts" only to subvert them with the subjective conclusions of a homiletic idiom, the words "God has two hands" also connote divine independence. With his "two hands" God seems able to establish the Kingdom alone. Moreover, the metaphor ascribes to God a sort of dual character and lends a sense of mystery or even

---

[27] *Ibid.*, 113.
[28] *Ibid.*, 117-188.

surprise to his actions. God's ways are not our ways, and so we wonder at times if his one hand knows what the other is doing.[29]

Such uncertainty introduces contradiction and conflict into otherwise rational systems of thought. True to form, however, what systematic theology eschews in the social Christian message, art will embrace. The following chapters attempt not only to supplement theological discussions with analyses of a parallel artistic tradition, they also try to demonstrate the benefits of reading both traditions together. What happens to the "intellectual paradox" of social Christian theology when the dramatic action of plots and the multiple connotations of poetic images become part of its vocabulary? Does the ambiguity diminish, or does it instead permit new meanings that perhaps are relevant even a century later? Using this approach, can we accept more easily Strong's words and conclude that, after all, God does have two hands? Moreover, can we learn how he uses them to

[29] Although it takes some liberties with the text, this reading of *Our Country* does raise an issue that pervades cultural expressions of the period from literary naturalism to sociological theory. In *The Rise of the Social Gospel* C. Howard Hopkins identifies the issue for social Christianity by pointing to a tension within the "ruling theological ideology of the day." If social Christianity sought to build the kingdom of God, he argues, it looked to "men of good will" and placed its faith in "the end result of an almost inevitable progress." At the same time that they "accepted an evolutionary kingdom of God," however, these social Christians also pursued an earthly kingdom and refused to admit the determinism implied by an evolutionary model. According to Hopkins, the Social Gospel not only promoted a sense of fate, it also "marched hand in hand with the muckrakers of the period" and joined in a Midwest "revolt of farmers against the entrenched plutocracy." Perhaps realizing the size of the free will-determinism dilemma he has introduced, Hopkins suddenly ends his discussion of the tension with an analogy: social Christianity during this period is something like an adolescent, "coming of age," but "not yet reached maturity." C. Howard Hopkins, *The Rise of the Social Gospel in American Protestantism, 1865 – 1915* (New Haven: Yale U. Press, 1940), 121-22. The analogy only highlights the depth of the problem. The free will - determinism dilemma has always been with us; what is interesting is the way cultures at different periods live with it. Here a "rich" literature of social liberalism helps Americans imagine an ontology that supports both horns of the problem. At a time when an enormous variety of changes—from staggering increases in the numbers of immigrants to the full operation of a transcontinental railroad to the emergence of corporate capitalism—introduced into daily reflection "the social problem," Christian ministers, theologians, writers and preachers tried to imagine a framework that could accommodate both the traditional rhetoric of individual salvation (free and predestined) and the growing body of references to change in a society they saw as subject to human influence and also (as one scholar of the period has called it) a "universe of force." Ronald E. Martin, *American Literature and the Universe of Force* (Durham: Duke U. Press, 1981).

shape the clay and write the tablets that constitute the imaginative patterns of our lives as social creatures?

1

"NOT OTHER, MORE": SOCIAL CHRISTIANITY AND THE RHETORIC OF WHOLENESS

> "Religion is about what is always slipping away. . . . This strange slipping away is no mere disappearance but a withdrawal that allows appearances to appear."
>
> Mark C. Taylor, *About Religion*

When Martin Marty defines social Christianity during the late nineteenth and early twentieth centuries by its quest for "a recovered sense of wholeness," he identifies a compelling theme within the movement. During this period Christians who were committed to a social "vision" challenged individuals to "'apply the Gospel's saving truths so much further as to bring the whole of a human life under their sway and the whole world into the Kingdom.'" For social Christians it "was always," Marty claims, "the *whole*."[1]

Although social Christians anticipated that God would grace life with a sense of wholeness in the near future, they nevertheless used images from the past to justify their expectations. The Kingdom of God will arrive, argues Jane Addams, when Christians apply to their lives the "age-long, time-tested, truths" of an ancient Gospel. As Marty points out, the social Christian quest for wholeness involved a "*restitutio ad integrum*" wherein advocates faced both the past and the future.[2] In 1887 Edward Bellamy dramatized this situation in his famous novel about future Americans who could explain their social conditions only by "looking backward" across the preceding century.

Social Christians from the period may have sought wholeness, but as their approach to this end suggests, unity for them presupposed division. Across a variety of genres—from poetry and fiction to magazine editorials, essays in theology and even cartoon art—social Christian writers discovered that the way to unity demands separation; that mapping the future Kingdom requires insight into the past; that Christians do not integrate elements anew but rather restore their original order. Drawing on the work of Eric Hobsbawm, Marty introduces the efforts of "moderns" during this period to develop a new "consciousness" by appealing to "'preindustrial custom and religion,'" the "'only spiritual resources at their disposal.'"[3]

What remains for those who follow Marty is to analyze specific works of social Christian writers like Walter Rauschenbusch, Washington Gladden, and Josiah Strong and to explicate in detail the tensions Marty finds between

---

[1] Martin E. Marty, *Modern American Religion*, vol. 1, *The Irony of It All, 1893-1919* (Chicago: U. of Chicago Press, 1986), 286, 288.

[2] *Ibid.*, 283-97

[3] Eric Hobsbawm, *Primitive Rebels: Studies in Archaic Forms of Social Movements in the Nineteenth and Twentieth Centuries* (New York: Praeger, 1959), 108. Quoted in Marty, *The Irony of It All*, 13.

past and present, tradition and novelty. Although this tension is implied in the trope Marty uses to organize his study of the period, irony, as well as in his attempts to correlate diverse elements of the movement such as the very practical Salvation Army and the more intellectual Social Gospel, its consequences remain largely unexamined. Even Marty neglects its implications, choosing instead to conclude his analysis of the "canopy" that seems to cover all social Christian attitudes and practices with references to its singularity. In Marty's remarkably detailed and even-handed study of the period, social Christianity nevertheless remains a unified and "creative movement" that serves as "one more novelty, one more contending party" for a "broken church."[4]

The need to recognize this tension within the movement is raised by many social Christian writers and artists who make it explicit in their works. The premier issue of the most popular social Christian paper on the east coast, *The Dawn*, identifies several sources of discord within its call to unity. "Our aim," writes editor W. D. P. Bliss

> is to favor all measures, to present all news, to aid all organizations, moving in our direction, especially to appeal to the Christian Church. Nationalists, Collectivists, Socialists, men of yet other names and no name, believe substantially with us. . . . We take no narrow stand; we welcome men of diverse views; we desire to see all sides.[5]

Although such a mission identifies and embraces tension, it is not necessarily consistent with the metaphors that frequently describe social Christianity throughout the magazine. "Dawn," for example, suggests a single moment that nevertheless threatens to dissolve into its constituent parts and all that they symbolize. The opening stanza of the poem by Charles H. Fitch entitled "The

---

[4] Marty, *Irony of It All*, 297.

[5] W.D.P. Bliss, "Salutamus," *The Dawn* 1:1 (May 15, 1889): 1. In addition to serving as editor for *The Dawn*, Bliss also preached and founded the Society of Christian Socialists in Boston.

Coming of the Dawn," which appears on page one of the first issue, illustrates this possibility.

> The new light is breaking-- God hasten it on,
> For many's the weary heart watching for dawn,
> And 'neath the long shadows that blacken the west,
> There's many a voice crying, there's many a hope
> dying
> In many oppressed.[6]

Fitch's poem asserts what Bliss claims in the opening paragraph of the same issue: "*The Dawn* is published in belief that society is awakening to new light upon social problems." The magazine "does not believe that it is yet day," Bliss insists, "but . . . that it is Dawn."[7] Through his poem, Fitch responds to the metaphor Bliss chooses when he describes the movement. In "The Coming of the Dawn" the poet asks God to "hasten" the new light because it will encourage the "weary heart." But as that light rises it does not illuminate or enlighten; rather, it casts "long shadows" that serve to "blacken" the "oppressed." Promising relief, the light leaves "hope dying."

Subsequent issues of *The Dawn*—especially those that print social Christian poets—explore the dichotomies that inhere in the rhetoric of "wholeness." The November, 1890 issue, for example, contains the poem "Two Prayers" by Julia Anna Wolcott, who writes of hope "born of that same sigh" as despair. Her poem claims that she can only "complete" her solitary "task" if she is allowed to "earn . . . peace through strife," a claim that divides both her "prayer" and her.[8] In a separate issue Katherine Lee Bates explicates the metaphor of the oak and its acorn which, like the earth itself, must "rendeth apart" before "that which thou wouldst be" can come alive. Bates' poem

---

[6] Charles H. Fitch, "The Coming of the Dawn," *The Dawn* 1:1 (May 15, 1889): 1.
[7] Bliss, "Salutamus," 1.
[8] Julia Anna Wolcott, "Two Prayers," *The Dawn* 2:7 (November 1890): 301.

begins with a reference to "the dawn's first silvery gleam" and ends with "the seed of . . . longing" that "breaketh" hearts.[9]

Frequently located in the most visible portions of Bliss's magazine, poems like those by Fitch, Wolcott, and Bates encourage readers to recognize that the social Christian message becomes both more profound and "practical" when delivered poetically. Following methods that are unavailable to essayists, social Christian poets help their readers perceive the "unimagined glories of the day" in the "midnight blackness changing into gray."[10] Because their language transcends references to theological or social scientific "processes," these poets relate the realities of "different men, different communities, different conditions"[11] to the quest for "One human family."[12]

The Dawn helps define social Christianity as an interdisciplinary movement. Not only poetry but book reviews, advertisements, and feature stories all advance the belief that imaginative works can dramatize in multiple ways the social Christian message. When Walter Rauschenbusch visits London in 1891 he reviews for the magazine an art exhibition at the Royal Academy and explains that he prefers those paintings in the exhibit that depict groups of individuals serving a single purpose because, through such service, they transform themselves into one identity. In a similar manner, when James MacArthur reviews the social Christian novels of Miss Katherine Pearson Woods, *Metzerott, Shoemaker* and *A Web of Gold,* he relates them to Edward Bellamy's *Looking Backward* and praises all three for their "Nationalism." According to MacArthur, the three works treat nationalism as a single ideal

---

[9] Katherine Lee Bates, "The Ideal," *The Dawn* 2:6 (October, 1890): 229
[10] Charles McKay, "Clear the Way," *The Dawn* 1:2 (June, 1889): 1.
[11] Bliss, "Salutamus," 1.
[12] *The Dawn* 4:1 (May, 1893): 34.

that resolves conflicts between individual and communal identities through an appeal to "power."[13]

Writers for Bliss's liberal-leaning *Dawn* were not the only social Christian advocates who sought to depict and reconcile competing identities. A more conservative, evangelical periodical, *The Ram's Horn*, published a similar message through the work of cartoonist Frank Beard. In numerous cartoons Beard compresses into single frames the same theme advanced by his literary counterparts (Figs.1 and 2). Whether Beard represents poverty or wealth, unsightliness or beauty, the "pattern" repeats itself: to "paint me as I am," is to discover that "every man has two natures."[14]

Two years after MacArthur names Nationalism as an ideal that synthesizes the competing identities depicted in social Christian fiction, T.C. Crawford published his social Christian novel *A Man and His Soul.* Set in Washington DC, the book is narrated by an unnamed newspaper reporter who meets within the city social scene a mysterious stranger, Mr. Arthur Harcourt. Harcourt, a visitor from the island of Nolos, is in the capital to further a "movement" that he insists "will be felt in all so-called civilized countries."[15] Beginning with the narrator and ending with the President of the United States and members of his cabinet, Harcourt demonstrates to his fellow characters in the text how they can "meet" and eventually converse with their own souls. Subtitled *An Occult Romance of Washington Life,* Crawford's novel uses the person of Captain Harcourt for two purposes. On the one hand, the Captain

---

[13] James MacArthur, "A Christian Socialist in Fiction," *The Dawn* 3:10 (January 1892): 3.

[14] Beard's early cartoons used characters to depict what he later referred to as "Old Yankee Notions," humor and satire that grew out of mid nineteenth-century situations. Although many of these cartoons were political and even set in Washington D.C., none shared with later social Christian artists the tendency to explore divisions within the self. Such inquiry expresses attitudes that prevail at the end of the century. Frank Beard, "Old Time Art and Artists," *Our Day* (February, 1896): 85-91.

[15] T.C. Crawford, *A Man and His Soul, An Occult Romance of Washington Life* (New York: Charles B. Reed, 1894), 125.

illustrates an ideal "oneness" and is able to insist that the "sole requirement" for a successful society is "universal brotherhood" under God. On the other hand, however, he also can point out that such unity involves a "chain of societies" with members who may "believe in one god or twenty." The "temples" built to these gods would invite "discussion" among members and encourage the "clash of intellectual strife"; however, to promote the variety needed for such exchanges society would have to organize only "the intelligent and well-to-do of this world." Captain Harcourt's plan for a social unity that follows the divine order requires that we eliminate "dead creeds" and the "husks of religion."[16]

A Man and His Soul is an excellent example of how popular social Christian literature explores and represents the tensions between a character's drive for "wholeness" and his or her corresponding need for division. Such tensions in the novel become more pronounced as the narrator meets his own soul and learns to ground social relations on one principle: "preserve your own individuality always."[17] This advice, which comes to the narrator from his soul, complicates Captain Harcourt's theories in two ways. In the first place, it bases the Captain's ideals of community upon the belief that "happiness is to be found only within one's self."[18] Therefore, although it supports the claim that "the world could be advanced when the individual could be made to reach upwards to his proper heritage," it does not help readers understand how to resolve the tensions between an ideal of communal oneness and the corresponding desire for individual satisfaction.[19]

In the second place, the advice not only places Captain Harcourt's theory on a foundation that contradicts its aims, it also "deconstructs" that foundation and identifies division and discord as a necessary part of all genuine

[16] *Ibid.*, 192-94.
[17] *Ibid.*, 209.
[18] *Ibid.*, 133.

quests for union. As the narrator studies a dark "Egyptian mirror" that sits in Captain Harcourt's room, the faint outline of a second "presence" begins to "steal across it like a mist."[20] Eventually the narrator's "soul" appears to him outside the mirror as his "exact counterpart," a figure "reclining in an easy chair [and] clothed in the modern dress of travel."[21] Readers learn that the journey to oneness entails what the novel calls "the complication of the double individuality,"[22] a phenomenon that is described by the Captain in a rather convoluted manner when he points out that: "Happiness is only to be found within one's self," but whoever discovers the self in the quest for happiness actually "conquers himself, and rises to his second self."[23]

The semantic difficulties involved in Captain Harcourt's advice are clumsy but, as Wesley Kort recently has argued, not uncommon to writers in the fields of religion or literary studies.[24] As a novelist of limited ability, T.C. Crawford has trouble expressing such ideas either didactically or dramatically. But so do others. Within social Christianity during this period, the author who is most sensitive to the possibilities raised by similar ideas is also the one who exerts perhaps the most lasting influence, Washington Gladden.[25] Gladden writes with a keen ear for the creative aspects of such difficult formulations. In

---

[19] *Ibid.*, 47.
[20] *Ibid.*, 24-5.
[21] *Ibid.*, 127.
[22] *Ibid.*, 130.
[23] *Ibid.*, 133.
[24] Kort's thesis is that we do not "adequately or accurately read . . . theological discourses" when we ignore the fact that they are related through "competition, opposition, and even repression." Wesley A. Kort, *Bound to Differ, The Dynamics of Theological Discourses* (University Park: Pennsylvania State U. Press, 1992), 1.
[25] According to Martin Marty, Gladden was nothing less than "the nation's best-known social Gospel liberal minister." As a pastor, essayist, theologian and novelist, Gladden's works reached both popular and "academic" audiences. He influenced the Church through his membership on the Committee of Direction for the 1912 Federal Council of Churches, and he affected political change as an advisor to Theodore Roosevelt and the national Committee of the Progressive Party. For more complete discussions see Marty, *The Irony of It All,* 213, and Donald Gorrell, *The Age of Social Responsibility: The Social Gospel in the Progressive Era 1900-1920* (Macon: Mercer U. Press, 1988), 151.

his essay on the incarnation he describes Jesus as "the Word" who embraced the "contrasts and contrarieties and antagonisms" of life not by transcending them but by signifying them. According to Gladden, Jesus combines the "unitary conception of a reality that is both "human and divine" with "an authority spiritualized."[26] Although he does not like the term "dual personality" to describe Jesus, Gladden nevertheless uses the phrase to convey what his friend, the poet Richard Watson Gilder, says more plainly in the same essay: that "Jesus Christ be a man" and "a God."[27]

Gladden's interest in "terms of a common nature" that Christians use to describe Jesus, and his dislike of "creed makers [who] try to set forth. . . faith in metaphysical terms," both lead him to support claims with examples from the poetic imagination.[28] As he writes about "The Incarnation," for example, Gladden uses poetry to correlate the Christian quest for unity with a corresponding tendency toward separation. When he searches for ways to express the dichotomy between wholeness and fragmentation, he turns to John Greenleaf Whittier, "the best theologian of them all," he says, and quotes extensively from the poem "Immortal Love, Forever Full."[29] To emphasize the peculiar difficulty of the Christian quest, Gladden chooses to begin his long excerpt from Whittier not with one of the many references in the poem to Christ's "present help," his "warm, sweet, and tender" presence, but with the troubling lament over our "vain . . . search." Gladden implies that, as Christians, we seek something that fragments our lives, and in this opening stanza images of physical distance between "heavenly steeps" and the "lowest

---

[26] Washington Gladden "The Incarnation," *Present Day Theology* (3rd. ed. Columbus, 1913), reprinted in Robert T. Handy ed., *The Social Gospel in America 1870-1920: Gladden, Ely, Rauschenbusch* (New York: Oxford U. Press, 1966), 169, 162, 156.

[27] *Ibid.*, 166.

[28] *Ibid.*, 164.

[29] *Ibid.*

deeps" introduce a series of references to distant entities that remind both poet and reader of God's position apart from us.

Gladden uses almost all eleven stanzas he quotes from Whittier to demonstrate how a desire to be "whole again" can produce "beds of pain." Jesus' "name," he notes, appears in our "first prayers" but also "burdens" the "last low whispers of our dead." Though his "presence maketh one," we can experience such unity only through multiple "clouds of white." The "Heavenly vine" and "earthly sod" of Whittier's imagined world develop the dichotomy introduced initially in stanza one through the two distinct and fragmentary elements of sky and sea.

By stanza seven "vine" and "sod" combine to produce "The flower of man and God." Thus in Gladden's essay, what the poet already knows the theologian must learn: that occasionally one finds "terms in which to express the difference" between mortal and immortal life without neglecting the experience of unity.[30] A proper theological vocabulary, says Gladden, describes the ways in which Jesus is "more, but not *other*."[31] The correct use of such terminology involves the rhetoric that virtually all scholars agree is central to liberal Protestantism and to the social Christian movement, the rhetoric of "immanence." When "men begin to think of God as immanent in creation," writes Gladden, "as revealing himself in the order and beauty of the universe, as the indwelling life of the world, as coming to the fullness of manifestation in humanity," then, he continues, "that old dualism [of human and divine] sinks out of sight."[32]

Gladden's words support a claim made in the most insightful study of the period, William Hutchison's *The Modernist Impulse in American Protestantism*. According to Hutchison, the idea of God's immanence

---

[30] *Ibid.*, 166. The Roman Catholic answer to this dilemma traditionally has been to introduce another literary term, analogy.

[31] *Ibid.*

"constituted" nothing less than "a new revelation" for social Christian theology.[33] Moreover, as he points out, ideas about divine immanence revealed to the movement the possibility of new "linguistic equipment" for late nineteenth-century believers. Contrary to Gladden's claims, however, this equipment did not enable the liberal doctrines of social Christianity simply to overcome the "old dualisms" of Christian theology. Rather, those dualisms remained potent within an alternative vocabulary. The concept of an immanent god allowed writers to reconceive the ways in which human and divine "natures" interacted in Jesus.

In the truly sacred realm, writes Gladden, "a divine nature and a human nature" are no longer "bound together" as two "distinct and separate entities." Instead, he argues, they are "blended and infused" to create a "union" that is more complete than even a shared "consciousness."[34] Although the words stretch traditional theological discourse, they do not of course overcome the divisions that Kort claims inhere within all theological discourse. Frequent references by Gladden to Christ's "humanity" or to his distrust of doctrines related to the virgin birth try to explain how a longing for "the whole" can surpass the persistent inclination toward disunity and fragmentation, but in the end the references fail to transcend the fact of division experienced by all social Christians of the period.

Although this desire to negotiate unity and separation is prominent in Gladden's theology, it finds an intriguing outlet in his fiction as well. In 1883 Gladden wrote a novel called *The Christian League of Connecticut*, which centers around two men in the small town of New Albion, Connecticut: The Reverend Theodore Strong, pastor of the Second Congregational Church, and Mr. Walter Franklin, manager and cashier at the First National Bank of New

[32] *Ibid.*, 158.

[33] William R. Hutchison, *The Modernist Impulse in American Protestantism* (London: Oxford U. Press, 1976), 100.

Albion. Together they persuade local ministers to join a Christian League Club and thereby create for the town "a little practical Christian union." The aim of this union is to stimulate "a consolidation of all sects into one church" and thereby establish an "organic whole" among all worshipping bodies. Events in the novel further this aim, and eventually the insights of the preacher and the banker culminate in a state-wide conference dedicated to this topic.[35]

Like so much fiction by lesser writers in the movement, Gladden's novel is also poorly developed, with static characters and too little dramatic action. Nevertheless, it does illustrate the assertion by Martin Marty that opened this chapter: that, for social Christians, "it was always the whole." The state conference that comprises one of the final scenes of the novel concludes with a message that is consistent with this preoccupation with wholeness, namely, that the "'*highest* ideal'" is to unify the churches and, according to those who participate in the gathering, failure to reach that goal condemns parishioners to "the evils of . . . denominational strife."[36] "'Blest be the tie that binds,'" the narrator states, and with that prayer he helps to elevate the idea of union to an ethical principle in the book.[37]

Although the climax of Gladden's novel dramatizes the value he places upon union, the voice he uses to narrate his story tends to promote a different ideal. The interdenominational conference that ends the novel is designed to produce a process that will unify parishes, but the voice that describes the conference and details the process significantly weakens the dramatic impact of the scene. Gladden insists upon using an omniscient narrator whose authority diminishes both the goal of Protestant union and its ethical foundations. Although the purpose of the novel may be to "let people once see how much

---

[34] *Ibid.*, 167, 157.

[35] Washington Gladden, *The Christian League of Connecticut* (New York: Century, 1883), 6, 10.

[36] *Ibid.*, 184-85.

[37] *Ibid.*, 9.

better and more Christian is cooperation than competition and conflict," readers in fact never "see" this point. The exchanges between pastors and parishioners that Gladden refers to as a way of illustrating cooperation come through a narrator who insists upon depicting in them a rigid hierarchy. By the time we reach the "postscript" of the book we cannot even distinguish between the voice of the narrator and the pen of author; we do not know which one pronounces the final words on "sectarian confusion," elevates the men "who are trying to bring a little order out of its confusion," and condemns those churches "that have no right to exist."[38]

When Gladden finishes *The Christian League* with a postscript that so thoroughly mixes his own voice with that of his narrator, he implies a connection between those tensions that dominate his narrative with his role as its author. By the end of the novel, therefore, the author—certainly the most prominent "emblem" of unity in any text—winds up fracturing the text and leaving readers confused about a number of things including, finally, who has been telling the tale. The scene at the state conference begins this process. As

[38] *Ibid.*, 192. The tension between ethical arguments for denominational unity and the narrative practices that promote division persist in Gladden's works. A prolific social Christian writer on matters of art and artistry, Gladden presents his aesthetic theories and interpretations in two texts: *The Relations of Art and Morality* (New York: Wilbur B. Ketchum, 1897) and *Witnesses of the Light* (Freeport: Books for Libraries Press, 1903). Although he sees no contradiction between the two fields, he insists that they are by no means equal. Beauty is to be desired and [the] right is to be chosen," writes Gladden and therefore ethical principles should guide our taste in art and literature. The "doctrine which overturns morality undermines the very foundations of art" (*Art and Morality*, 15). But in *The Christian League of Connecticut* Gladden's aesthetic approach undermines those ethical principles that determine his thesis and shape his theme. Gladden's insistence that "there is a hierarchy of affections and the active powers" in human life requires the evaluative vocabulary he uses throughout *Art and Morality*. Certain art is "diviner," "higher," "nobler," "loftier," worthier," and "highest" (*ibid.*, 9, 18, 19, 21, 54). Embedded in these terms are comparisons and contrasts that sharpen critical approaches but do not necessarily promote unity. Moreover, when he fashions a narrative from his principles he creates a voice that excludes all but his point of view. Gladden's approach violates the very rule for "great art" that he borrows from Ruskin and advocates in *Witnesses of the Light*: do not promote that which narrows or excludes ideas but that "which tends . . . to enlarge and ennoble the mind" (*Witnesses of the Light*, 256).

the character of Walter Franklin, bank manager and cashier, addresses the crowd, he quotes letters he has received from various people in the novel. Gladden's "postscript," added immediately after that chapter, not only continues Franklin's practice of presenting letters but actually cites Franklin and raises the same issues as his narrator. At this point distinctions between writer and narrator become extremely difficult to make. The situation grows more complicated when readers realize that Gladden published his "postscript" as a separate piece in the September, 1883 issue of *Century* magazine. Reported in *Century* as an account of actual events, the story of New Albion churches that appears in *The Christian League* suddenly becomes for readers both fact and fiction. Read in the light of its conclusion, therefore, Gladden's novel could be interpreted as a "prescript" to the evidence of social reform outlined in its closing pages. Did it happen or didn't it? Was unity reached with the help of an author who feels he must "blot out" not only certain churches but even the fictional elements of the story he tells?[39] In this novel, by one of the most important ministers of the social Christian message, the answers are ambiguous.

Writing about social Christian unity does not necessarily occasion experiences of it. Perhaps one reason is that, for social Christians, writing itself seemed to occasion an experience of fragmentation. At one level T. C. Crawford's novel is about the act of writing. When the book opens, all we know of the narrator/protagonist is that he "had formerly, for years, filled the post of a social correspondent in Washington."[40] When it ends, we learn of his decision to leave the city and complete a "record" of his work with Captain Harcourt. In between we read that the narrator's life is best understood as a

[39] Gladden, *The Christian League of Connecticut*, 192.
[40] Crawford, *A Man and His Soul*, 9.

"story," complete with "chapters" and a "conclusion" and staged frequently within "the interior of a library,"[41]

The narrator's role as a writer becomes increasingly significant as the novel unfolds. A "society" writer, the unnamed individual should produce prose that focuses his attention on public topics. But "society" writers typically write about the private matters of their subjects; they report gossip about personal issues, and Crawford's character is no exception. At one point in the novel the President of the United States refuses to see him because he fears that what he says in private will become public: "He would rather give up seeing you," an aide says, "than to run the risk of having a word about it in the newspapers." These are the same "papers" the narrator reads in the Senate gallery as he waits for two public figures to confront one another about a personal scandal. Acts of writing in this novel become difficult to categorize; the aims of one practice are subverted by the realities of a second.[42] The narrator discovers that it is difficult to write about reform with a comprehensive and "ideal" social vision when private scandals interrupt, divert, and divide the attention of authors and readers

But *A Man and His Soul* dramatizes a difficulty that is far more profound. In this novel acts of writing symbolize the search for identity, and therefore the breakdown of a unified approach to prose implies a corresponding split within the self. In Chapter 21, entitled "I Invoke, Alone, My Soul and Receive Some Directions for Spiritual Development," the narrator sits "up in front of my writing table" and gazes at two items that Crawford correlates by their proximity to one another: Captain Harcourt's dark Egyptian mirror and "a mass of blank white paper." Staring at the mirror and holding his pen above a sheet of paper, the narrator is "thrilled by the sensation of a foreign control of my arm." His muscles respond to "the direction of an unseen influence" and,

---

[41] *Ibid.*, 152.

after a "few clumsy marks [are] made," suddenly "words begin to form" and the narrator is able to read a single phrase: "Don't believe all you see."[43]

Immediately after this experience, the narrator's second self appears to him in the mirror and his quest for wholeness seems over. Yet the words he has written during this apparent experience of union with his soul raise doubts about what in fact has been made "one." Like other attempts to produce a unified discourse in this novel, the act of writing here seems to diminish the very intention that motivates it. In this case the result of what the book calls "automatic writing" is not a growing certainty that the narrator is "whole" or at one with his soul but a direct caution: "Don't believe all you see." Intended to bring the narrator and his soul closer together, the act of writing raises doubts about the ability of individuals to experience and describe with confidence even the most familiar spiritual presence, their own souls. Whether anyone can ever experience Jesus directly or through a social setting becomes, for the social Christian writer, a fresh problem.

Such doubt threatens to dissolve the plots of social Christian narratives into a collection of discreet episodes. Gladden's autonomous "postscript" and Crawford's uneven chapters read this way. Even the most popular social Christian novel ever written, Charles Sheldon's *In His Steps*, suffers from this tendency. However, Sheldon's text surpasses others within this genre because it transforms the weakness of fragmentation into one of its genuine strengths. Uncertain about the ability of individuals to experience Christ as present, Sheldon frames the dilemma of disunity differently. Rather than create a vocabulary that would define wholeness in terms of Jesus' identity and actions, Sheldon eliminates the need for such declarative statements and chooses to pose a question. According to *In His Steps*, the challenge is not to describe in

---

[42] *Ibid.*, 206, 137, 70.
[43] *Ibid.*, 207.

theological terms the figure of Jesus as a unified Man-God but more basically to wonder, using our imaginations, “what would Jesus do?”

2

FILLING IN THE BLANKS
ABSENCE AND PRESENCE IN THE WORKS OF CHARLES SHELDON

In the last scene of a novel by Charles Sheldon entitled *The Crucifixion of Phillip Strong*, a wealthy industrialist named William Winter stands before the fresh grave of the protagonist and reads his tombstone.

PHILLIP STRONG.

Pastor of Calvary Church, Milton.

"In the cross of Christ I glory,

Towering o'er the wrecks of time;

All the light of sacred story

Gathers round --"

As he turns and walks away from the site he notes the final "incomplete line" and comments that "Yes, it is better so. We must complete it for him."[1]

[1] Charles M. Sheldon, *The Crucifixion of Phillip Strong* (Chicago: A.C. McClurg and Co., 1894), 266

The scene is significant for several reasons. In the first place, it concludes the novel and directs the attention of readers to certain themes. It reminds us, for example, of the way Sheldon compresses time in his narrative and uses texts such as letters, sermons and, in this case, poetry within the book. As the final scene it also helps to bridge this novel with the phenomenal 1896 best-seller that follows. Too often critics have read *In His Steps* without any reference to Sheldon's lengthy bibliography, which includes two novels and thirty stories prior to 1896 and five novels afterward. The death of the Christ-like Phillip Strong that ends the first story prefigures directly the death of the tramp who wanders into the lives of Reverend Henry Maxwell and his parishioners during the opening pages of the second tale.

In the course of concluding one novel and anticipating the action of a second, this scene proves to be significant for a third reason as well. Through it Sheldon identifies the principle that motivates virtually all aspects of his fiction, the principle of absence. From *The Crucifixion of Phillip Strong* to *In His Steps*, from *The Redemption of Freetown* to the *Miracle at Markham*, time and again readers find themselves in positions similar to that of William Winter: they are faced with texts that they must complete in order to grasp their full meaning. In every case Sheldon uses absence to define his social Christian message.

The most obvious example of this principle is the refrain "what would Jesus do?" that runs throughout Sheldon's corpus. As Wayne Elzey points out, *In His Steps* alone repeats the question over 200 times, and that is after Sheldon uses it as the subtitle of his book.[2] It appears in various guises in almost every other novel as well. "I wish you would with me," Phillip Strong asks of his congregation during an early sermon, "try to see if you think Christ

---

[2] Wayne Elzey, "What Would Jesus Do?" *In His Steps* and the Moral Codes of the Middle Class, *Soundings* 58 (Winter, 1975): 121-37.

would actually say what I shall say in his place."[3] In the 1899 novel *Miracle at Markham*, nothing less than "a baptism like that of the Holy Ghost at Pentecost" occurs when the Congregationalist minister John Proctor preaches on the topic "What Would Jesus Do If He Were a Member of a Church Today?"[4] Outside of his fiction, Sheldon is quite explicit about relations between the question and the actions he depicts. In an essay originally titled "The Law of Christian Discipleship," Sheldon writes that "discipleship means no less today than it did in Christ's own lifetime." "The discovery of electricity, the building of . . . telegraph and telephone lines . . . the inventing of printing presses and type-setting machines, the modern life of humanity, with its daily papers . . . its scientific energy—all has not changed in any smallest particular the relation between Jesus and a human being."[5]

Through this query, or some version of it, the literary and the theological dimensions of Sheldon's work repeatedly intersect and readers are encouraged to imagine answers that essentially "complete" each narrative. At the end of *In His Steps*, for example, Henry Maxwell asks "has not the time come for the dawn of the millennium of Christian history?"[6] Until readers answer that question, the story remains unfinished. Sheldon repeats this narrative technique in other works. In the last lines of the novel *The Redemption of Freetown* he presumes that Jesus would do as the citizens of Merton have done, and so he questions readers: "Shall the world ever be redeemed in any other way?"[7] At the close of the *Miracle at Markham* he continues to consider what Jesus would do in a contemporary setting and, through his character John Proctor, he inquires of readers whether the

---

[3] *Ibid.*, 22.

[4] Charles Sheldon, *The Miracle at Markham* (Chicago: John H. Ulrich: 1899), 96-98.

[5] Charles Sheldon, "The Law of Christian Discipleship," *The First Christian Daily Paper and Other Sketches* (New York: Street and Smith, 1899), 80.

[6] Charles Sheldon, *In His Steps* (New York: Books, Inc., nd.), 243.

[7] Charles Sheldon, *The Redemption of Freetown* (Boston: United Society of Christian Endeavor, 1898), 64.

preceding action has provided evidence to answer the question: "Was not Christ's yearning prayer being answered at last?"[8]

Wayne Elzey correctly asserts that the questions Sheldon asks in his works function as mnemonic devices. They are "homilies" in the sense that "they teach by challenging individuals not only to recall significant events in the life of Jesus, but more importantly to remember and to think through, again and again and at various levels of experience, the classes, categories, and principles according to which reality is organized."[9] Elzey emphasizes the "experience" of reading the questions and the epistemology that results from encounters with the text. According to Elzey, *In His Steps* provides readers with nothing less than "a paradigm—a model or blueprint for thinking." They accept Sheldon's tendency to repeat a question like "what would Jesus do?" because the question functions as "myth," suggesting that "there is only one world, operating according to the same principles from top to bottom."[10]

Elzey's analysis is the first to take seriously the religious content and function of the text by relating both to the questions that dominates so much of the narrative. But like others who have analyzed the book, Elzey too focuses on the "content" implied by the question or, if you will, on the answers that readers are bound to provide in order to experience Sheldon's message as a genuine "paradigm" or "myth."[11] Like others, his reading ignores the question *per se* and neglects the influence of the rhetorical device on a wide range of narrative elements, especially those two that Sheldon carefully correlates, plot and style. To read the novel in terms of the question it poses over 200 times does not necessarily result, as Elzey maintains, in a "religious code." Instead it

---

[8] Charles Sheldon, *The Miracle at Markham*, 314.

[9] Wayne Elzey, "'What Would Jesus Do?' *In His Steps* and the Moral Codes of the Middle Class," 465.

[10] *Ibid*, 470.

[11] *Ibid*, 484.

calls attention to the need or desire for such a code. In other words, the question emphasizes the absence of any "codes" within the narrative.

Elzey's 1975 conclusions depend upon an argument Paul Boyer makes four years earlier. Although they disagree about the role of religion in the novel—for Boyer the book is a psychological study "concerned only minimally with religion" while for Elzey it depicts a genuine "spiritual quest"—both argue that Sheldon has structured his text around certain pairings of characters, actions, and ideas.[12] Boyer reads *In His Steps* as a text "concerned, almost obsessively, with certain psychological and emotional problems troubling the American middle class at the close of the nineteenth century."[13] Central to those problems are the dual attitudes of middle class characters toward the proletariat and toward all that represents "the masses." "On the one hand," writes Boyer, the middle class "projects upon these alien laborers the menace of unbridled individuals, social irresponsibility and potential violence . . . . But on the other hand," he continues, "the presumed intensity and turbulence of lower-class life offer the middle class a possible escape from the emotional cul-de-sac in which it finds itself." Contact with laborers in settings as diverse as saloons and prayer meetings produces in certain middle class characters both disdain and "a capacity for experiencing life more deeply."[14]

Unlike Boyer's concentration on one pair of middle class attitudes toward the proletariat, Elzey's focus is much more complex and elaborate. Not only does Elzey explicate in the novel tensions within the middle classes and describe those tensions as symptoms of deeper social forces, he also charts the double meanings of these forces in ways that depict positive and negative dimensions in each. For example, social action in the plot of *In His Steps* depends upon a variety of characters but most notably upon the forces

[12] Elzey, "'What Would Jesus Do?'" 468; Paul S. Boyer, "*In His Steps*: A Reappraisal," *American Quarterly* 23 (Spring 1971), 62.

[13] Paul S. Boyer, "*In His Steps*: A Reappraisal," 62.

generated by two types: "the masses," who occupy places like "the Rectangle," and "the status seekers," who include characters like Rollin Page, Milton Wright, Donald Marsh and Rachel Winslow's cousin, Felicia Sterling. The masses suffer from undefined social roles and excessive intimacy with one another, but they can boast of their common sense and good fellowship. By contrast, status seekers in the novel have rigid roles and tend to be anti-social. Sheldon balances such "vices" with virtues that emerge when status seekers act in "typical" ways. Within the plot, even rigid social roles lead to exemplary social figures, and the tendency toward impersonality stimulates in status-seeking characters a strong sense of individuality.

When Boyer describes the ambivalent attitude of the middle class toward a proletariat that both degrades and saves others, and when Elzey maps the dual roles played by all social groups depicted in the novel, both emphasize the presence of certain defining qualities and experiences that organize Sheldon's plot. Elzey discusses "dress, food, law . . .mental processes, musical tastes, motives, sexual habits, etc." in order to show not only the way each social group directly influences action in the novel but also to demonstrate for readers that these groups exhibit specific "codes" that tend to locate them in one of two distinct areas. "All [social] oppositions" in the novel, argues Elzey, "can be reduced to the basic contrast between "nature" (the lower class) and "culture" (the upper class)."[15] Boyer would concur, for he too focuses his attention on those distinct expressions of class in the novel, i.e. alcohol among the proletariat and cultured sensibility among the upper classes. According to Boyer, the upper class character of Rachel Winslow, for example, "restores threatening situations to tranquillity" among the masses simply by "the total impact of her presence."[16]

---

[14] *Ibid*, 78.
[15] *Ibid*, 477.
[16] Boyer, "*In His Steps*: a Reappraisal," 10.

But neither the tangible elements of a material culture nor the physical presence of certain characters drives the plot of *In His Steps*. Boyer makes much of Rachel Winslow's singing to an impoverished and rough crowd during a tent meeting at the Rectangle. According to his analysis, when Rachel sings, she "subdues lower class passions" and tames into "harmlessness" the "wild beast" that constitutes her audience. He is correct, her physical presence does leave a deep impression upon her audience, and she makes a similar mark during other, more intimate encounters such as the time she spends with the former prostitute Loreen. But ultimately what matters in the novel are the very things that seem to be "missing," experiences of intangible or spiritual reality that motivate characters to act.

The scene at the Rectangle is instructive. Rachel sings, but her song is not about God's presence. Rather, it describes an experience of absence. "Savior, I follow on / Guided by Thee, / Seeing not yet the hand/ that leadeth me." Through the hymn, the singers celebrate the power of the absent God, and they confess the constructive dimension of their own incomplete nature. "Hushed be my heart and still / Fear I no further ill, / Only to meet Thy will, / My will shall be."[17]

Sheldon confirms the importance of absence to the scene by depicting the response of two central characters who are suitors of Rachel Winslow, Jasper Chase and Rollin Page. As suitors, both of these men are defined by their desire for Rachel and by the fact that neither one "possesses" her. She is, in other words, absent to both. The first suitor, Jasper Chase, desires Rachel to such an extent that, in this scene, his otherwise "greatest longing"—to be an author—is "swallowed up" in his "thought of what [Rachel's] love might sometimes mean" to him. Through his desire for her, he becomes separated from a portion of himself. The second suitor, Rollin Page, stands at the

---

[17] Sheldon, *In His Steps*, 165.

margins of the same tent service, literally "over in the shadow outside," longing to enter into the meeting as a way to reach Rachel. Separated from her, he nevertheless is "swayed by the power that [she] possessed" and longs for her all the more.[18]

Rollin experiences physical, emotional, and spiritual alienation as he stands in the shadows of the tent, but eventually he wins Rachel's love. By contrast Jasper, who is much closer to Rachel during the service, trades the intangible "rewards" of her love and a deeper communion with the Holy Spirit for the tangible remuneration of his career. Eventually he does choose to write novels, but for two specific reasons: "money and fame."[19] Boyer is right to focus on this scene as instrumental to developing the plot lines that are essential to these characters.

Although his emphasis on the scene is well-placed, Boyer neglects to interpret the most powerful motivating factor in the passage: absence.[20] True, Rachel Winslow does sing before various "workers" at the Rectangle; however, the group that matters most in her performance is not the one in front of her but the one she thinks about during her song: "the flippant, perfumed, critical audiences in the concert halls."[21] These middle and upper middle class status seekers are the ones in the novel who must ask the question "what would

---

[18] *Ibid.*, 65.

[19] *Ibid.*, 140.

[20] The omission also prevents Boyer from finding in the text evidence that could help readers understand in part the aesthetic value of middle class ambivalence in this and other Sheldon novels. Boyer takes the novel to task because, unlike a social Christian work such as Edward Everett Hale's *How They Lived in Hampton* (1888), Sheldon's book fails to present "a quite explicit blueprint for industrial cooperation based on Christian principles." From an artistic perspective it is difficult to see how a revision like this would improve the value of the novel. Middle class characters like Rachel Winslow, Jasper Chase, and Rollin Page are interesting in part because of their ambivalence, not in spite of it. Turning them into spokesmen for an "explicit blueprint" limits the few dimensions they already possess. Nor would such a change improve the quality of characters from other novels such as *Malcolm Kirk* (1906) or *Born to Serve* (1900). In virtually all cases Sheldon has crafted characters with some range of human emotion and complexity; they display certain creative contradictions. Boyer, "*In His Steps*: A Reappraisal," 66.

[21] Sheldon, *In His Steps*, 65.

Jesus do?" and their absence from this particular scene helps readers to complete a transition to the next. As the episode at the Rectangle ends, the preacher Henry Maxwell also is not thinking about the crowd to which he just spoke but about "his church members," the ones who own the "saloons" and the "property" that mark the Rectangle area as a "festering sore" on the social body of Raymond. He continues to think of them as he returns to his study in the following scene to ponder their proper response to the persistent refrain: "what would Jesus do?"

Boyer and Elzey both argue that "middle class" beliefs, attitudes, and ideals constitute the principal subject matter of this novel. Yet neither acknowledges that, as an identifiable social group, this "class" is largely absent from the book. Despite opportunities to depict groups of middle class characters in settings such as Sunday services (chapter one) or the theater (chapter twenty one), Sheldon chooses to group them as a collection of individual characters who, as he points out in Chapter 13, share a bond based to a great degree on "things which they could not talk about."[22] When Henry Maxwell meets with middle class characters like Virginia Page, Edward Norman, and Alexander Powers during "after-meetings" at the First Church, he joins a group who experience "fellowship" with one another but also a sense of growing "estrangement" from their class.[23] They have ceased to function as a middle class group.

The absence of a clearly defined and well-represented middle class shapes the episodic plot of the novel. Unlike *The Crucifixion of Philip Strong*, wherein contingents of middle and upper middle class parishioners serve as catalysts for much dramatic action, *In His Steps* focuses on individual characters who are bound together by their reference to the central question, "what would Jesus do?" One consequence of this difference is that *The*

---

[22] *Ibid*, 112.

Crucifixion of Phillip Strong builds to a definitive, easily recognized climax, that moment in the Milton Calvary Church when Phillip backs up against the Church wall and, "with outstretched arms, almost covering the very outlines of the cross," dies a symbolic crucifixion.[24] *In His Steps*, by contrast, lacks such an obvious climax. In its place, Sheldon gives readers a narrative that concludes by increasing the number and scope of certain elements that recur throughout the text. As the narrative moves from Raymond, Kansas to Chicago, various aspects of the story seem to expand and fill the scene.

For example, in a typical chapter from the novel—one set in Raymond— the narrative poses approximately seven to ten questions. Some of these questions are versions of the refrain "what would Jesus do?" Others address related matters. More important than the content of the questions, however, is their number. As dramatic action in the novel climaxes, Sheldon's narrative poses questions with much greater frequency. By the time readers reach the last two chapters, thirty and thirty-one, they find no fewer than thirty-three and fifty-one questions, respectively, in each.

Clearly the practice of posing questions constitutes an important stylistic technique for Sheldon, one that he associates directly with action and plot. This technique establishes the significance in the text of certain climactic moments. For example, chapter thirty, which is set in a Chicago "Settlement House" for the unemployed and homeless, dramatizes a series of questions put to the Reverends Maxwell and Bruce and to the Chicago Catholic Bishop. In this chapter the question that prompts the most discussion comes to Maxwell from an unemployed carpenter who wants to know "what Jesus would do in my case." "I've tried every way I know to get a job," he exclaims. "What

---

[23] *Ibid*, 112-13.
[24] Sheldon, *The Crucifixion of Phillip Strong*, 264.

would Jesus do if He was out of work like me?" According to Rev. Maxwell, "this is a question that brings up the entire social problem . . ."[25]

In this passage, which raises several opportunities for the narrative to clarify if not answer the question "what would Jesus do?" Sheldon chooses instead to complicate the query with multiple voices and approaches. The scene presents a range of characters who respond to the carpenter from the audience and give voice to various social theories of the day. A man named Carlsen, for example, offers a socialist response; a second man provides the perspective of single-tax proponents; a third assumes the role of anarchist. Although he offers no clear alternative, Sheldon supports none of these theories and, as the chapter closes, the carpenter's question remains unanswered. As if to avoid formulating an answer, Sheldon sees to it that, at this moment, everyone present becomes lost in songs performed by Rachel Winslow, who has followed her own path from Raymond to Chicago. His strategy works and even the Bishop, who has listened carefully to the entire exchange, muses only about "the Kingdom" coming "quicker" when "preached . . . by consecrated prima donnas and professional tenors and altos and bassos."[26]

Taken together, chapters thirty and thirty-one offer readers the most impassioned prose in the novel. But because their passion comes to us negatively through multiple questions that have no definitive answers, they convey both the absence of important information and the strong desire for it. "No one," writes Sheldon of the Settlement House meeting, "had any true conception of the feeling pent up in that room that night."[27] Reverend Maxwell senses it, and for the first time in the novel we hear his "heart" praying. Reverend Bruce also recognizes it, but when he hears the carpenter

---

[25] Actually, as phrased by the carpenter, it is no less than five questions, a point that illustrates Sheldon's ambivalent attitude toward the subject matter. Sheldon, *In His Steps*, 227.

[26] *Ibid*, 232.

speak he simply bows his head and laments a "human problem" that had become "tragical." In this setting, the refrain of the novel—"what would Jesus do" becomes a "terrible question."[28]

Episodic, replete with questions, and deeply concerned to convey a sense of absence, these final chapters do not just summarize and conclude the novel, they represent it in a compact, almost intense way. As such, they call attention to themselves, to their prose and the way Sheldon composes. The novel ends with Rev. Maxwell's vision of the refrain "'what would Jesus do' inscribed over every church door . . . written on every church member's heart" and carried as a "banner" by all "Endeavor Societies." As part of the climax to the novel, this phrase describes not only church doors and banners, it also refers to the subtitle of the book itself. In this way the question directs readers back over the preceding action to consider how Sheldon's prose arrived at this conclusion.

Other episodes from these final chapters compliment this reflective movement. When Rev. Maxwell speaks in chapter thirty to a congregation at the Chicago Settlement House, he is "reminded of his first night at the Rectangle" back in Raymond.[29] Rachel Winslow's singing provides a second reminder, as does Maxwell's sermon delivered in the very next chapter. From a public "prayer service that in its impressions repeated the Raymond experience" to Maxwell's private "rehearsal" of the "events of the day," action in the climactic chapters suggests movement back over a drama that has already transpired.[30] The repetition suggests one of Sheldon's moral conclusions to the book: that when characters experience certain settings again and again they learn how to walk in His steps.

---

[27] *Ibid*, 225.
[28] *Ibid*, 228.
[29] *Ibid*, 231.
[30] *Ibid*, 240.

What is true for Sheldon's characters is also true for his readers, for when they too review actions from those earlier scenes they learn how to walk in His steps. For readers, though, Sheldon's phrase has multiple referents. In the first place it refers to the dramatic actions of characters who are trying to imitate Christ by walking with him. In the second, it refers to the novel itself, to the text that carries the phrase as its title. Given the context in which Sheldon originally read this and other novels, it is fair to say that he sought to establish a direct relationship between drama and text, believing that, when one learned how to interpret his novel, one also discovered how to walk with God.[31] Finally, the phrase refers to a different text altogether, the one Sheldon quoted to obtain his title, the Bible. As the opening chapter of his book indicates, the phrase comes from 1 Peter 2:21. "For to this you have been called, because Christ also suffered for you, leaving you an example that you should follow in his footsteps."

The Biblical passage introduces a context that is crucial to Sheldon's prose in this novel and others. The first letter of Peter is addressed to churches in Asia Minor that the author feels must become like "newborn infants" (2:2). It opens by remembering the resurrection, the event that early Christians believed carried the past into the present and beyond. Moreover, frequent references in the letter to baptism encourage Peter's audience to recall a more personal event, one that not only formed them as Christians but, in some cases, occurred under the direct guidance of the Apostle Paul. Having reviewed, repeated, and thereby represented a way of life that Jesus established when he

---

[31]Without exception Sheldon composed his fictions for his congregation at the Central Church, Topeka, Kansas. His novels are homilies, delivered primarily to young adults in his parish during Sunday evening services. Typically, Sheldon read one chapter each week and, consistent with his narrative techniques, chapters usually ended with a question. Sheldon concluded twenty-three of his thirty-one chapters of *In His Steps* this way. Even when his works were serialized in Social Christian journals like *The Ram's Horn*, they retained their homiletic character and format.

walked the earth, 1 Peter ends with a call to its audience to "remain firm" in their convictions.

None of these points is lost on Sheldon, who read the entire Bible as a child with his parents and brother no less than six times before he left South Dakota for Philips Academy in Andover. The most provocative context for Sheldon's choice of 1 Peter 2:21, however, is the one that is most immediate to that passage: "If you are patient when you suffer for doing what is good," writes the author of the letter, "this is a grace before God" (2:20). To walk in Jesus' steps is to suffer as he did: specifically, it is to suffer in ways that will limit severely social contact. "Be subject to every human institution for the Lord's sake," insists the author, even if it means assuming the lowliest social position (2:13). "Slaves," he admonishes, "be subject to your masters with all reverence, not only to those who are good and equitable but also to those who are perverse" (2:18).

Clearly, for the author of 1 Peter, remembering Christ and remaining firm in Christian convictions requires that one also return to the lowliest social position. Gentile slaves, who neither fear nor avoid the whip—for there is no "credit" for being "beaten" when you have done wrong—should remain slaves. Grace follows "whenever anyone bears the pain of unjust suffering" (2:19). When we remember Christ we travel back into slavery; we diminish ourselves in order to walk in His steps.

The logic behind this traditional Christian formula controls virtually all aspects of Sheldon's prose, including the process of writing. Certain points emerge time and again as the author removes the framework for change. Take away the traditional plot, and you have a collection of episodes that repeat the same message. The editorial process by which one reduces the text to such key points is extremely important. It is the means of making things "absent" so that readers can admire and exalt what remains.

The most succinct outline of this process appears in the brief sketch by Sheldon entitled "A Newspaperman for a Week."[32] "The daily papers print too much," Sheldon writes. "Half of it might never be printed, and the other half should be thoroughly revised before the public sees it." He goes on to quote a claim from the *Congregationalist* that a "'newspaper containing only the news and the really vital thought of the day compressed into a short space is among the successful enterprises of the future which some genius will perpetuate'"[33]

Sheldon dramatizes such a "genius" in a character from *In His Steps* named Edward Norman, editor of Raymond's newspaper, *The Daily News*. As editor, Norman commits for one year to "run the paper strictly on Christian principles," and he agrees to go to press only after he has asked the question that motivates all actions in the novel: "what would Jesus do?" Although one would suppose that such a commitment would result in an expanded paper with a more comprehensive coverage of religious life and events, the opposite in fact is true. Printing a daily paper that reflects "Christian principles" results in much smaller editions. Gone are stories that cover perceived violence such as prizefights; gone are advertisements from tobacco companies and liquor stores; gone is the Sunday edition. In the eyes of its readers, Norman's "Christian" paper is defined by two related characteristics: what it leaves out and what it repeats as a result of having been so thoroughly edited.

These same characteristics define Sheldon's work in various genres. For example, the way Sheldon uses moments of "silence" in his most prescriptive social Christian novel, *The Redemption of Freetown*, reveals how narrative "actions" in his fiction can repeat experiences of absence. Sheldon introduces that novel with a reference to the atonement of Jesus. More than an example of self-sacrifice, Christ's atonement presents a model that readers

[32] Charles Sheldon, "A Newspaperman for a Week," in *The First Christian Daily Paper*.

[33] *Ibid.*, 29.

should follow in their own lives. We repeat it, and in so doing we copy an act that forces the self to become absent, as one "who gave Himself." The rhetoric of silence that permeates the text follows from this idea, and it allows Sheldon to develop his creative attitude toward absence. In this novel, "silence" operates according to the same logic as the definitive act of Christian sacrifice: it describes an active state through attitudes that are truly passive. As Sheldon says, silence marks an "inward passion" and "shows plainly how deeply [characters] feel." In *The Redemption of Freetown*, "stillness" is "deep and full of meaning."[34]

It is essentially the same in texts ranging from Sheldon's "sketches" to his autobiography. In the short piece entitled "Six of Him," for example, Sheldon describes a minister who is so busy with parish work that he discovers himself miraculously cloned five times. Consistent with his narrative techniques in his novels and other longer works, Sheldon connects repetition in this piece with absence. According to the plot, the minister cannot be cloned or "repeated" until he in some way is diminished. Only when the pressures of the job drive him out of his town spiritually and mentally "exhausted" do his other "selves" appear to complete his work.

In addition to evidence drawn from novels, sketches and essays, one work, Sheldon's autobiography, provides readers with a paradigm for understanding the interplay between absence and repetition in his prose. Written in 1925, Sheldon's *Life Story* opens with a scene he calls "real history." Similar to the "real news" he believes newspapers should print, "real history" distinguishes itself by its value: it consists of a story worth repeating. Of this particular scene of "real history," Sheldon writes that "I do remember now, and perhaps I shall always. . . ." His memory enables him not only to

[34] Sheldon, *The Redemption of Freetown*, 35, 23, 43.

recall the scene clearly but, as he remembers, to repeat his tale for readers who are intended to see it as evidence of God's presence.[35]

What Sheldon repeats, however, is a story of God's presence that is controlled by images of absence. The scene takes place at Sheldon's childhood home in South Dakota; in it his father is at the bottom of a deep well that the family recently has dug. Water begins to seep into the hole, and all members of the family taste it and pronounce it good, not only for what it contains but also for what is absent: "no alkali." In the process of completing the well young Charles and his brother must raise a sixty-pound wooden bucket full of mud out of the hole. During this process the brothers watch in horror as the bale suddenly breaks and sends the bucket falling sharply back into the hole. Sheldon has only one thought at the sight: "Father's killed."[36]

But Stewart Sheldon is not killed; he is not even injured. In this scene, the anticipated event does not happen. In fact, nothing happens in the tale, except that the bucket knocks the hat off Sheldon's father. When the family takes an opportunity to stop and thank God, they thank Him for something that did not occur, for the absence of an event. The story Sheldon remembers and repeats is about the way an event failed to occur; it relates how his father did not die. Yet for Sheldon that absence constitutes the presence of something very important: God in "real history."

This incident, which holds a preeminent position at the beginning of Sheldon's autobiography, identifies a paradigm by which many of his works should be read. Set around a well, itself an image of absence, the scene dramatizes the tensions that motivate so much of Sheldon's work. As his father stands at the bottom of the well, he clears the dirt away with a "shooter," "waiting for the water to seep in" (20). The action is significant for the

[35] Charles Sheldon, *Charles M. Sheldon, His Life Story* (New York: George H. Doran, 1925), 21.
[36] *Ibid*, 19-20.

interplay it describes: remove the dirt, and the water, which is so valuable to life on the Dakota prairie, comes to you. In many ways Sheldon does the same thing when he writes, creating "spaces" in his texts to convey a sense of "absence." Like the incomplete tombstone read by William Winter at the end of *The Crucifixion of Phillip Strong*, this sense of absence encourages readers to discover a "presence" that is uniform, constant, and eternal.

Before readers can claim to recognize substantive social Christian themes and programs in Sheldon's works, they need to understand the role of absence in his texts, especially as it influences plot and style. For Sheldon, the greatest tale told is the one in the New Testament wherein the "Christ of God" is found "exchanging gain for loss," choosing absence over presence.[37] That New Testament tale is told as a "sacred story," one that, through its lack of substance, illuminates as does a "soft clear light." If readers would see by this light, they must understand that the Bible "discloses" its subject by taking away the darkness, literally by "removing closure." In such a light the reader recognizes a peculiar personal and social glory, one that steals life with a cross, diminishes time, and leaves us without our God. And thus, according to the elements of Sheldon's prose, we celebrate our subsequent social Christian slavery. It would take some of Sheldon's contemporaries on the prairie and further west to connect such slavery to the image of a God who is truly masterful in his otherness.

---

[37] Sheldon, *The Crucifixion of Phillip Strong*, 267.

3

SOCIAL CHRISTIANITY AND THE PROBLEM OF THE WEST

> "I will only say that the growth of society resembles in some respects the growth of a plant or an animal; and that is a statement which nobody can deny."
>
> W. Gladden, *Social Facts and Forces*

> Within twenty years after the Mayflower anchored in Plymouth harbor, there were several prosperous settlements on the Connecticut River . . . . And ever since that day the tide of immigration has been flowing steadily westward—westward—over the Appalachian range, down the valley of the Ohio, along the borders of the Great Lakes, across the teeming prairies, over the Rockies and the Sierras to the Western shore. That mighty movement of people westward, westward, which began long before Abraham took up his journey from Haran to Canaan, has been going on ever since. . . ."
>
> W. Gladden, "Migrations and Their Lessons"

Part of what makes Sheldon's story of the episode at the well a paradigm for his subsequent work is its "seamless" quality. It is a memory of origins that makes youth its primary character. It describes the relationship between parent and child using the classic psychoanalytic image of a father who is almost killed by his son's negligence. And it places its central action, the digging of an empty well, in a setting that is remarkably appropriate. Perhaps no region in the country compares with the Dakota plains as a location devoid of features, and it is here, under a vast firmament, that Sheldon's tale has its genesis.

Because the term "social" implies locations outside the individual, social Christianity by definition is concerned with "settings" for human interaction. Moreover, as Sheldon's story indicates, at times social Christians identify those settings with specific regions and permit them to influence various aspects of an otherwise religious message. One way to read the above quotations from Washington Gladden, therefore, would be as separate instances of the vague, sometimes abstract sociological theses that too frequently became part of social Christian essays, novels, and sermons. A second way, however, is also possible. Read together, these passages raise an interesting new problem, one that emerges when readers contrast the regional references in both quotes. Gladden's "society" in the first passage is decidedly urban and "eastern"; it describes the growth of New York, Boston, Chicago, and other metropolitan centers that expanded tremendously under the pressures of immigration and industrialization. By contrast, the second passage refers to the western United States, also populated by a "tide of immigration" yet suggesting no metaphors of plant or animal growth to describe its advances. If eastern urban centers progress according to the laws that govern individual organisms, western states seem to follow the rules of history and are subject to the hand of "Providence" as it manages the aims of historical sequence.

The distinction is clear and somewhat puzzling. It seems more common to reverse these descriptions and refer to history when discussing the eastern states and to the language of organic growth when describing the West. After all, the roots of the American Jeremiad are in New England and, as most Americans knew by 1897, the grandeur of the West was attributed almost exclusively to its natural phenomena—the height of the Rockies and the sweep of the Plains. Yet despite the more "typical" order of these descriptions, Gladden chooses a different approach.

There are many contexts for Gladden's observations, but the most immediate are essays themselves. The first is taken from a piece titled "The Church," the second, "Migrations and Their Lessons," comes from a sermon Gladden preached on the Letter to the Hebrews 9:8. At first glance, therefore, both contexts suggest the importance of religion for understanding Gladden's claims. Closer scrutiny confirms and refines this connection: "the Church" of the first essay is the "true integrating force in society"; the "omniscient Ruler" who manages Providence in the second passage is a social god who "enlists more or less directly all the great nations of modern history."[1]

The implicit and explicit distinction Gladden draws in these texts between east and west are informed therefore by a social Christian context. Moreover, other advocates of a social Christian position from this period tended to make similar distinctions as they interpreted eastern societies as single, integrated organisms and western societies as products of highly determined historical patterns. When two writers as different as Josiah Strong and Walter Rauschenbusch, for example, seek to illustrate the chief attributes of urban living in the east, they employ language about the body. According to Strong, eastern cities represent the "nerve centers of our civilization." They grow like cells "doubling and doubling again" their populations, and eventually they suffer a "paralysis" that leaves them "prostrate" and "exhausted."[2] Rauschenbusch makes a similar point through his use of a "parable" that compares eastern city dwellers

---

[1] Washington Gladden, "The Church" and "Migrations and Their Lessons in *Social Facts and Forces* (New York: G.P. Putnam's Sons, 1897), 181, 192, 205.

[2] Josiah Strong, *Our Country*, ed. Jurgen Herbst (Cambridge: Harvard U. Press, 1963), 171, 186.

to angleworms dug and forced to live in a can. As such they are like "organisms taken out of their natural surroundings;" crowded together, they becomes a single "mass," "infested and rotting," and it is this body of people that falls prey to "many of the most deadly diseases, especially tuberculosis."[3]

If Strong and Rauschenbusch use metaphors from organic life to describe the urban centers of the east, they turn to the language of historical development to describe the ways in which western America has grown. "In our country," writes Rauschenbusch, "the land in its vastness and abundance, its variety and wealth, has been one of the most sanitary influences in our national life." The ensuing discussion in *Christianity and the Social Crisis* of a "vast" American landscape, recognizable to early twentieth-century readers as a reference to the geography of the west, shifts immediately into a historical narrative that begins with the American Civil War and moves backward through Cromwell's England, to the Roman Empire, and eventually to ancient Israel and the struggle between Jacob and Esau. According to Rauschenbusch, "next to life itself the greatest gift of God to man is the land," and such a gift requires an account of its origins.[4]

In his fascination with the west and "Western supremacy," Strong frequently discusses the unique quality of time in any understanding of that region. "Ten years in the New West are, in the results, fully equal to half a century east of the Mississippi." Even when he has an opportunity to develop a notion of the west as a single, living organism similar to his descriptions of eastern territories, Strong cannot help but infuse the metaphor with meanings that require historical references. At one point, for example, he asserts "the West is to-day an infant." But he then goes on to insist that his readers recognize the infant as "the young Christ" whose star "has ever beckoned the wealth and power of nations westward." The west may "one day be a giant," says Strong, but its

[3] Walter Rauschenbusch, *Christianity and the Social Crisis*, Robert D. Cross, ed. (New York: Harper Torchbooks, 1964), 227-28.

[4] Rauschenbusch, *Christianity and the Social Crisis*, 221-225.

deepest significance rests in the fact that "since prehistoric times" populations have moved steadily toward it "as if driven by the mighty hand of God."[5]

Used in a wide variety of "texts," both verbal and visual, this rhetoric about the west complicates two widely-accepted generalizations about social Christianity: that it neglected the past in order to emphasize the future of God's kingdom and that it portrayed God exclusively as immanent within creation. Accurate to some degree, both of these generalizations neglect the defining characteristics particular regions had upon the movement. They pertain more directly to social Christianity as practiced in east-coast, urban centers where the call to work for God's Kingdom elicited a corresponding belief in the willingness of the divine to establish himself in and through "modern" social structures. When social Christian advocates discuss life in these regions, for example, they talk about locating churches in the heart of large metropolitan areas. Like Walter Rauschenbusch, who ministered to those in need in the Hell's Kitchen area of New York City, these advocates were convinced that under such conditions Christians could "enter into the joy and peace of the Kingdom" simply "by laboring for it."

When the setting changes to include images of life in other areas, particularly those areas "west of the Mississippi," the corresponding interpretation of God also seems to change. The Kingdom of God remains a central tenet, but theologians, writers, sociologists, novelists, and painters are far less confident about their ability to "enter into it." They dwell on its past far more than its future, and they experience it first as a manifestation of God's difference or distance. In "western" settings, the God of social Christianity is decidedly "other."

One reason for this sense of separation is that for many associated with the movement, the west was "other." For Nadine Tilford, protagonist of Nina

[5] Strong, *Our Country*, 18, 39-40.

Ellison's 1897 novel *Nadine: Romance of Two Lives*, the west resembled a "supernatural dream," a "mystical," "enchanted land." On a journey west to meet the man of her dreams in California, Nadine passes through the entire landscape of the western United States and writes accounts for her local Kentucky newspaper of what she sees in places like the Colorado Rockies and Utah's Great Salt Lake. Unlike the physical or even moral degeneration of more established areas east of the Mississippi, the west appears in Nadine's accounts as a Biblical landscape—"the summit of the universe"—where once warred "Beelzebub's hosts and heaven's archangels."[6]

The choice of Biblical rhetoric by Ellison and her protagonist to describe the western landscape calls attention to the importance of language in the descriptive process. Because the west was unfamiliar to many of their readers, social Christian writers did not simply describe the region, they used words to create it for them. Novelists, for example, frequently demonstrated this point by reporting the correspondence of those characters who traveled west. For Nadine Tilford, the west to which she journeys certainly is a physical location; but the fact that she reports her visit through written correspondence calls attention to the role of language in mediating an image of this place. The narrator does not directly represent Nadine here; instead, she offers us letters from Nadine in which her heroine crafts the environment with words.

Similar situations occur in two other novels, Charles Sheldon's *Richard Bruce* and Jessie Pounds' *The Ironclad Pledge*. In *Richard Bruce* the main character interrupts his budding career as a Chicago writer and novelist to travel to the Dakotas where he will help ailing relatives—people named, significantly, the "Wests"—on their farm. More than twenty-five pages of the novel are dedicated to recording the cycle of letters exchanged between Richard and his friend Tom,

---

[6] Nina E. Ellison, *Nadine: Romance of Two Lives* (Nashville: Gospel Advocate Publishing Co., 1897), 164, 166.

and when the protagonist returns he immediately assumes a position on the weekly Chicago-based paper, *The Christian.* In *The Ironclad Pledge* Jessie Pounds devotes far less space to the letter-writing activities of his central character, the aspiring poet Phil Darrington. Nevertheless, Phil's letters, which he sends to his fiancé from the small western town of Greenville, provide the principal means by which the author contrasts the "bright world" of "eastern" society with the "life of toil and . . . privation" that characterizes the west.[7]

The ways these novelists employ language about the west illustrates points made recently by both Diane Dufva Quantic in her study of Great Plains fiction and J. Gerald Kennedy in his book about American writers and another location that inspired much fiction, Paris. The western writer, asserts Dufva Quantic, "uses language to establish the meaning of place."[8] In this literature one "meaning" of the west is that it represents an alternative to the realities of the east. However, as Dufva Quantic's assertion makes clear, the alternative is linguistic and therefore consists of a vocabulary of words that generate meanings out of their relationships with and differences from one another. When an eastern writer like Walter Rauschenbusch, for example, refers in 1907 to "the land in its vastness and abundance," his readers know that he is not writing about the crowded conditions in the eastern United States but about that portion of the country his fellow easterner, Josiah Strong, claimed could contain much of the "civilized" world.

In his discussion of Paris as a setting for early twentieth-century American literature, J. Gerald Kennedy uses the categories of contemporary critical theory to make a similar point. He observes that "one cannot compare an 'actual' place with its literary representation, since there is literally no 'place' apart from an

---

[7]Jessie H. Pounds, *The Ironclad Pledge: A Story of Christian Endeavor* (Cincinnati: Standard Publishing Co., 1894), 125.

[8] Diane Dufva Quantic, *The Nature of the Place, A Study of Great Plains Fiction* (Lincoln: U. of Nebraska Press, 1995), 155.

interpreting consciousness. The only possible comparison for the critic is thus between a personal, readerly concept of place (perhaps informed by knowledge of an existent site) and a textual, writerly image." The essential difference between these two linguistic entities, Kennedy maintains, "lies not in the relation between real and fictive environments but between textual scenes and the symbolic experiences of place which they inscribe." Through the use of literary techniques like letter writing, late nineteenth-century social Christian novelists create opportunities for the "rhetoric of the west" to serve as the principal connection between the "readerly concept" of the land and its "textual . . . image."[9]

That phenomenon is not limited to social Christian novels. *Our Country* uses language about the west to join fixed notions of that region with certain national ideals. "The West is characterized by largeness," writes Strong in the opening lines of chapter three. "Mountains, rivers, railways, ranches, herds, crops, business transactions, ideas; even man's virtues and vices are cyclopean. All seem to have taken a touch of vastness from the mighty horizon." Through his description Strong is able to associate the west with a wide range of features that address the principal concerns of Americans during this period. Not only natural phenomena but technological advances ("railways"), economic opportunities ("business transactions"), intellectual insights ("ideas"), and moral character ("virtues and vices") are all described here as "western." Strong even goes on to claim that, because of their "largeness," certain "stories" also must be considered western.[10]

Novelists, theologians, and artists from this period were joined by still others in their attempts to "stretch" language and thereby describe the west. In 1896 Frederick Jackson Turner claimed that "the West, at bottom, is a form of

---

[9] J.Gerald Kennedy, *Imagining Paris: Exile, Writing, and American Identity* (New Haven: Yale U. Press, 1993), 5.

[10] Strong, *Our Country*, 27-28.

society, rather than an area."[11] Theodore Roosevelt had asserted three years earlier that the frontier operates like a Biblical "wilderness" where "life is reduced to its elemental conditions."[12] Earlier still Clarence Dutton had chronicled the geography of the region and mapped its formations with names like "point Sublime," "Temple of the Virgin," Vishnu's Temple," and "The Cloisters."[13] Through their choice of vocabulary, all of these writes sought to describe a land and, by extension, a nation capable of meeting certain key challenges because of characteristics they called "western."

Unlike many of their counterparts, however, writers who expressed an interest in Christianity and its social function frequently shared a theological reason for describing realms of human experience as "western." They wanted to establish the sacred quality of not just the land but also its defining qualities, specifically, the history it revealed and the future it promised to support. "The two Dakotas," writes Strong, "might be carved into half-dozen kingdoms of Greece; or, if they were divided into twenty-six equal counties, we might lay down the two kingdoms of Judah and Israel in each."[14] Implicit in Strong's claim is not only that the physical dimensions of the west enable it to contain other lands but that its mythical status also allows it to hold the past. In this case, the past includes the three lands most directly responsible for the origin of a global western civilization, Greece, Judah, and Israel. Like paintings by George Harvey in Iowa or Olof Grafström in Oregon, Strong's words encourage us to understand the vastness of the west in terms that are both geographical and temporal.

---

[11] Frederick Jackson Turner, "The Problem of the West," *Atlantic Monthly* LXXVIII (September 1896), 289-97; reprinted in *American Thought and Writing: The 1890s*, ed. Donald Pizer (Boston: Houghton Mifflin, 1972), 156.

[12] Theodore Roosevelt "In Cowboy Land," *The Wilderness Hunter* (New York, 1893) 412-24; reprinted in *American Thought and Writing: The 1890s*, ed. Donald Pizer (Boston: Houghton Mifflin, 1972), 178.

[13] Clarence Dutton, *Tertiary History of the Grand Canyon District*, United States Geological Survey, Director J.W. Powell (Washington: Government Printing Office, 1882), 57-60, 140-56, 177-82.

As used by social Christian advocates, language about the west joins place and time in ways that complicate our usual understanding of theology during this era. Typically, when writers have discussed the way social Christian advocates thought about God during the period, they have insisted on two points. The first is that social Christians believed God works progressively and will establish his Kingdom in the near future. The "whole movement had something of a utopian cast" writes Robert Handy in his now classic presentation and analysis.[15] Although Handy qualifies his statement when he asserts that social Christian advocates did not believe "in automatic or inevitable progress, for they normally saw progress as conditional upon man's response to divine leading," his work nevertheless reinforces the unambiguous claim that, above all else, social Christianity "heralded the coming kingdom." According to Handy, "the spokesmen for the social gospel expected that, through the efforts of men of good will, the kingdom of God would soon become a reality, bringing with it social harmony and the elimination of the worst social injustices."[16]

Related to interpretations of a "progressive" God, the second point made frequently by those who study this movement is that its God was characterized as "immanent" within world processes. Many historians and cultural critics, for example, have pointed out that, according to social Christian thinkers, Darwin's theories of evolution and natural selection did not constitute valid arguments for the workings of a random biological sequence. Rather, they indicated processes that were controlled by the divine and directed toward a sacred purpose. Because social Christian writers of the time were supported by the works of others from a wide variety of fields, most readers have concluded that social Christianity held

[14]Strong, *Our Country*, 28.

[15] Robert T. Handy, *The Social Gospel in America 1870-1920: Gladden, Ely, Rauschenbusch* (New York, Oxford U. Press, 1966), 10.

[16] *Ibid.* Handy's thesis follows from the writings he chooses to anthologize in his collection. Limited to three writers, Washington Gladden, Richard T. Ely, and Rauschenbusch, Handy's book collects pieces that address the role of eastern, urban social Christians in hastening the coming of the Kingdom of God. None of his examples address the west as a topic.

uniformly to convictions about the immanence of God's presence in the world. For social Christian advocates, "cultural immanentism," writes William Hutchison, "ratified the actual presence of God in Humanity."[17]

The theological foundation for both of these points is doctrinal. Social Christianity, as Hutchison argues, ratified God's presence through an appeal to one particular Christian doctrine: the Incarnation. However, as the quotes that open this chapter indicate, when social Christians imagine God's Kingdom in a decidedly "western" environment, the appeal changes. No longer does the Incarnation provide the controlling set of metaphors for the social Christian enterprise. Instead, advocates turn to the Exodus story for terms that both describe and lend meaning to the "plains" or "western" experiences of social Christianity.

By neglecting language about or images of the west in this movement, students fail to grasp the multiple ways its understanding of history also shapes its theological assumptions. When social Christians consider life in regions "west of the Mississippi," the Kingdom of God remains a central idea; they discuss its future, however, far less than they do its past. According to many, the primary responsibility of the Church in a western setting is not to promote the future Kingdom but to continue traditions begun in the past. Time and again social Christians conceive of and represent society in the western United States as an extension of a Biblical Canaan. The westward march of people onto the plains and beyond continues a movement "which," in the words of Gladden, "began long before Abraham took up his journey from Haran. . . ." As the heroine of Nina Ellison's *Nadine* discovers, a journey through this relatively unsettled frontier does not mean that one finds only new opportunities to be realized sometime in

---

[17] William R. Hutchison, *The Modernist Impulse in American Protestantism* (New York: Oxford U. Press, 1976), 4.

the future; it also means that one "invades the past" and comes to terms with a God who, in many respects, remains identified with a distant history.[18]

Such distance does not occasion talk of God or the Kingdom as immanent within the Church and society. Rather, it suggests that God may be intimately connected to the social world but that he nevertheless is also different from it. If God is imminent within western society as a result of his work within history, he also is decidedly distinct from it and "other." Like the figure of Yahweh in the Exodus tale, this God leads his people to the mountain but reserves the top for himself. The 1895 frontier novel *Evangel Ahvallah or the White Spectrum* by Josephine Barton illustrates this point. Set in a small prairie town, the novel opens with a brief description of the region that deliberately locates the church fifteen miles away from the town and the pastor one and a half miles distant. The description of course is accurate insofar as the members of many small communities had to travel some distance on Sunday to hear a preacher who divided his time between different parishes or missions. More interesting, however, is the way Barton's description of the setting supports action within the narrative. For example, within the first ten pages the main character, a little girl named Evangel, has a "vision" of "a luminous Globe" that approaches earth and touches it at the western horizon. Evangel recognizes its difference from the earth, and the narrator notes that the "orb" constitutes "a moving, living WORLD" unto itself. It is a world of light, "superior to the earth," and in her vision Evangel sees herself actually stepping onto "this glorious realm" and breathing its "beautiful atmosphere."[19]

Barton's description focuses the reader's attention on the differences between the two worlds, and it provides what she calls a "metaphysical deduction" to explain an otherwise physical separation between the church and the

---

[18] Ellison, *Nadine*, 163.

[19] C. Josephine Barton, *Evangel Ahvallah: or, The White Spectrum* (Kansas City: the Author), 1-10.

community. Many social Christian novelists dramatize the sense of "otherness" that characterizes the frontier experience of religion. John Howard, who runs the boarding house in an 1895 novel called *The Story of a Canon*, feels alienated from the Church and does not attend despite the fact that he is a deeply spiritual figure in that book.[20] When Charles Sheldon sends his protagonist Richard Bruce to the Dakotas, he allows the principal religious voice in the text to remain with the Rev. John King, a Chicago-based preacher whose influence actually draws Richard and his family back to the city for religious reasons.[21] Jessie Pounds' *The Ironclad Pledge* is precisely what the sub-title indicates, a story of the "Young People's Societies of Christian Endeavor." In it the Society comes to "the brisk Western town of Greenville" and settles in the Church, which is "a plain little wooden building on a narrow street at the very border of the town."[22] Action centers on ways to manage the discrepancies between a church that is both physically and spiritually distant from Greenville and citizens of the town.

Visual artists who portray the western church in social settings contribute to this sense of "otherness." Regional painters such as George Harvey of Iowa; Olof Grafström, who painted landscapes and constructed altarpieces throughout the west and midwest; Christian Eisele of Oregon, Colorado, and Utah; Harry Learned, who worked in both Lawrence, Kansas and Denver; Denver and Pueblo artist Joseph Hitchens: all produced works that, among other things, represent the Church in late nineteenth-century western society. Where they locate religious figures and buildings within their compositions reveals a great deal about the way they perceive the social role of religion. Their works helped to shape how both east and west-coast advocates of a social Christianity imagined the sacred or, to use the language of the movement, the Kingdom of God.

---

[20] Beveridge Hill, *The Story of a Canon* (Boston: Arena Publishing Co., 1895), 56-7.

[21] Charles Sheldon, *Richard Bruce or The Life That Now Is* (Chicago: Advance Publishing, 1898).

[22] Pounds, *The Ironclad Pledge*, 18

Learned's depiction of *Robinson, Colorado*, Grafström's *View of Portland*, and Hitchens' *Admission of Colorado to the Union* are good examples. Learned distinguishes the church in his landscape painting of this small Colorado town primarily by its color and location. A bright white structure, the church sits higher than all other buildings in the horseshoe-shaped village that occupies the floor of a broad valley. Even the mine that sits on the same plane as the church and is much larger is not elevated in this way. Moreover, Learned separates the Church from the town by placing it at the edge—in that space where the wilderness of a forested hillside ends and the spare, tree-less valley begins. The white of the church is matched by the snow on the tops of distant mountains, a connection that further distinguishes the church from the town while also suggesting the origin of its authority.

The paintings by Grafström and Hitchens make similar connections (Figs. 3 and 4). In *View of Portland*, Grafström places his church building in line with both the hazy and distant image of Mt. Saint Helens and a group of fallen trees in the foreground. The sublime character of the former joins the power associated with the falling of the latter to form a vertical axis that not only crosses but also transcends the horizontal lines created by the river and railroad. Located on the vertical axis, the church, already the highest point within the town, is both central to society and lifted out of the social setting as part of the more "privileged" natural realm.

The same pattern of propinquity and distance defines the theme of Hitchens' *Admission of Colorado to the Union.* Like Grafström, Hitchens balances the earthly and the sacrosanct; in this case he places the mythical "Miss Columbia" in proximity to the heavenly grandeur of the capital building, which is remote in the clouds and divine in its "otherness." In an interesting way, however, Hitchens expands his message to include not only a negotiation of "near" and "distant" religious images but also "high" and "low" modes of artistic expression.

The capital and the landscape seen beyond are "classical" in their appearance. By contrast, the people gathered before the arch are stiff and graceless in their ceremonious poses, two-dimensional counterparts to the carved wooden figures one finds in so many displays of "folk" art from the period.

This dichotomy within religious emblems that are central to society yet also transcendent of the social order parallels the dual role of the church in other regional paintings. Furthermore, it also introduces a tension that, in this period, is characteristic of social Christian works, particularly when they invoke the vast territories of the western United States. To a social Christian minister like Washington Gladden, it seemed that the movement of people westward onto the plains and into Colorado, Utah, and California suggested pairs of external "forces"—"attractions and propulsions" he called them—to which was added a series of "conflicting motives," not only "the love of life," "the love of liberty," and the "love of change," but also "hunger and fear," "impatience of restraint," and "the greed of gold."[23]

Regional painters such as Learned, Grafström, and Hitchens are joined by others to form a group of artists, all of whom produced canvases that negotiated the nearness and distance of the divine by depicting the Church as both part of and separate from western society. Like so many novelists who wrote about the region and made much of churches symbolically located "at the edges" of their fictional towns, these painters repeatedly represented churches that both dominate their social settings and threaten to disappear into the ever-encroaching wilderness.

A particularly striking example is George Harvey's large panorama entitled *View of Burlington* (Fig. 5). In that work Harvey paints no fewer than six spires in the Iowa city, suggesting the importance of religion for the life of the community. Yet he reserves the most outstanding location in the scene— a hill outside the city that overlooks all of its elements—for one of the most distinctive features in the work, a solitary church. Moreover, he surrounds that church with the branches of a dying tree that stands in the foreground. Such a combination creates an interesting sequence for viewers whose eyes begin by looking at the details of the town and move gradually to the edges where the lone church seems both powerfully autonomous on the hill and threatened by the tree.

Combine these images, which are located on the left side of Harvey's canvas, with that of the river, which appears opposite on the right side, and viewers discover that the artist has framed the town with a group of very traditional Christian symbols: the church, the tree (often used as a synonym for the cross), and the river of baptism. To frame the city of Burlington this way is to provide a visual commentary on the social organization that appears within the frame. It is, in short, to accomplish with paints what numerous social Christian writers used words to create: a critical perspective on changes associated with the "modern" world, depicted here through the railways and factories that occupy large portions of the canvas.

In a manner very similar to social Christian theologians and novelists from the period, George Harvey depicts the constitutive elements of social reform from a Christian perspective. And like others who imagined what such reform would involve outside the large urban centers of the east coast, Harvey gives viewers a set of images that are mixed and, to a great degree, contradictory. The Church building that dominates the city is also dominated by the tree; the tree itself, which stands as the natural antithesis to the industrial development of the town, has as its artistic parallel in the picture those smokestacks that line the river; and the river, which serves as a mode of transportation for industry, is also painted as a means of escape from this growing midwest metropolis.[24]

---

[23] Gladden, "Migrations and Their Lessons," 183-84.

[24] Viewed from the south, however, the only means of escape we see goes north, against the current and toward the origins of the waterway. In other words, to leave behind all that

The tension within a western experience of social Christianity may reflect the consequences of a much deeper uncertainty about identity in this region. According to Richard Etulain's recent study of the twentieth-century western American imagination, the "struggle of the West to find its identity" in a nation begun in the east results in a "major tension" that runs throughout the fiction, history, and art of and about this area.[25] Rauschenbusch perceived this tension when he wrote about the homestead system for distributing western land. Although homesteading exhibited certain "salutary" features, "we have come to the point," he argues, "where the elements of injustice in the system will begin to menace us."[26] True to form, his analysis of this western American practice leads him into a discussion of history, specifically the distant past of ancient Rome and the influence of Roman law on modern ideas about private property. For Rauschenbusch, Rome provides an appropriate comparison because it offers a profound example of social tension within a system of land distribution. In Rome, the communal practice of apportioning land to citizens of the Republic evolved into imperial conquests under the legal codes of the empire. According to Rauschenbusch, therefore, one "chief cause for the fall of Rome," ironically, "was embodied within Roman law."[27]

When social Christians showed an interest in a society "of the land" in settings like the plains or western states, they preached about a Kingdom of God that was fraught with tensions. A future possibility that nevertheless was heavily determined by the past, this western example of the Kingdom was presented as a force present both inside and outside the social sphere. It took its leading characteristics from an experience of God at the horizon, both approaching and

---

Burlington seems to represent, one cannot float easily into a future Kingdom; one must struggle on a journey backward, as it were, into the past.

[25] Richard Etulain, *Re-Imagining the Modern American West, A Century of Fiction, History, and Art* (Tucson: U. of Arizona, 1996), xviii.

[26] Rauschenbusch, *Christianity and the Social Crisis*, 224.

[27] *Ibid.*, 223-24.

receding, and like the world Evangel Ahvallah encounters in her vision, it came to us like a "line of forest" that "changed places with the sky," growing by turns both darker and then lighter."[28] "Far out on the plains," the Kingdom of God begins to resemble the land around and under it, a place Nadine Tilford describes as both a "dead world" of "vast solitude" and "man's Eden."[29]

An interesting example of this tension from a plains publication helps to illustrate the point (Fig. 6). Between May, 1906 and August 1910, the state of North Dakota published *North Dakota Magazine*, which was "established for the purpose of setting forth the resources and advantages of North Dakota and of attracting immigration." In its efforts to describe the state to outsiders, the magazine represented all aspects of social life in the area, including the religious dimension. Between May, 1906 and August, 1910, it published photographs of churches on forty of its pages. Of those forty pages, only six contain images of a single, isolated church; 85% of the time photographs of churches appear grouped with other images—hospitals, schools, community centers, etc.—to create an impression of a religious entity thoroughly enmeshed within the social fabric.

Because the format used to present these photographs is the collage, viewers see North Dakota churches two ways. By one viewing, churches appear to be partners in the community. The proximity of church photographs to others suggests that religious faith operates as a principal element of society, building and sustaining the Kingdom from within the social sphere. By another viewing, however, churches—indeed all social elements—appear to function autonomously. The collage format creates an impression of separate and distinct social units. Discreet photographs imply individual objects that simply are placed next to one another for aesthetic reasons. Any sense of a social "context" in this case could be arbitrary and the church may be just one element among many. According to this view, the Kingdom of God would be the province of an

[28] Barton, *Evangel Avallah*, 9

institution that is present to the community from the outside rather than the outgrowth of a church that functions within social spheres.

The interesting point is not whether one view is correct or even more accurate but that two are possible. In more recent works, the spiritual writer and Benedictine oblate, Kathleen Norris, has distinguished this region for the contradictory impulses it generates in its inhabitants. The tendency to look to the land and its people and see both harshness and beauty results, according to Norris, in a corresponding experience of religion as "a tension I can't name."[30] Two additional images of religion in a social context from this period and place support Norris's more general claims. Although *The Lay Preacher* by Hebjörn Gausta, painted in 1884 (Fig. 7), takes its title from the figure in the center of the work who is addressing those around the table, clearly the painting is deeply concerned with the seated audience and therefore with the social dimension of the religious gathering. The title alludes to this complicated relationship by suggesting that this "man of God" is a "lay" individual who is not easily distinguished from those around him. In this painting the only distinguishing features are that he stands and speaks, two gestures that could be duplicated by others in the group.

Pairs of images that recur across the canvas increase the sense of tension that Gausta conveys through his title. Eight figures comprise the audience, and they come two by two, starting with the two women on the left side of the picture who represent the emotional extremes depicted here. The woman by the window is completely at peace; by contrast, her counterpart, who is seated at the table, is the most troubled figure in the work. As viewers look around the table they notice other pairs that illustrate similar tensions. The two old men are seated, but one leans forward without his spectacles while the other, who seems more reserved, pulls back but wears his glasses. Two women of very different ages follow. The

---

[29] Ellison, *Nadine*, 163-64

[30] Kathleen Norris, *The Cloister Walk* (New York: Routledge: 1996), 11.

older one looks puzzled if not angry with the preacher; the face of the younger appears blank, and the viewer surmises she may not be listening at all. The vague, almost indistinct faces of the last two figures on the right side are in stark contrast to the original pair. One cannot even recognize their gender, let alone their emotional states.

All eight are seated around a table that contains a "pair" of spectacles. These call attention to the dual role of vision in this painting. In one respect, certain evidence suggests that the eyes are unreliable instruments here and that, to repeat the words prompted by the dark mirror in T.C. Crawford's novel, you can't necessarily believe what you see. The most intent listener to the word has removed his glasses; at least one half of the members of the audience do not make eye contact with the preacher; there are numerous shapes and images that the viewer cannot discern. All of these points call into question the value of visual experience in this work. In another respect, however, vision is extremely important to *The Lay Preacher*. The removed spectacles are not simply located on the table, they sit atop a copy of the Bible. Grief is associated with blindness as the woman to the right of the table covers her eyes. The light from the window, which bathes the most peaceful listener, also enables others to read from the Scriptures that lay open on the table. One point of Gausta's work seems to present within the picture discrepancies that suggest the multiple and conflicting aspects of a single identity as well as the positive and negative sides of certain defining characteristics. The combined effect is a composition that dramatizes the tensions within a "plains" or "western" experience of social Christianity.

Students of American social Christianity could select a number of individuals to represent the diversity and tensions within the midwestern, plains, or western manifestations of the movement. Included on their lists, however, surely would be the congressman from Nebraska who ran for President three times and eventually became Secretary of State under Woodrow Wilson, William

Jennings Bryan. As even his nickname suggests, the "Great Commoner" lived a public and private life that was characterized by the kind of contradictory impulses we have described as typical of this movement. Made somewhat notorious late in his life for his role as the voice of conservative religion in the Scopes trial, Bryan nevertheless introduced many pieces of progressive legislation throughout his career. Deeply evangelical in his faith, Bryan was concerned with a variety of issues related to a more social Christianity and actually spoke to the convention of the Federal Council of Churches in 1914. A private man with respect to personal matters, Bryan was a gifted orator who addressed a wide range of groups, from national political conventions to Chautauqua participants. That last tension within his character is what cost him so dearly during the Scopes trial, for although his words at the trial were offered with great personal sincerity, they lacked the focus and clarity of those delivered by defense attorney Clarence Darrow. Their exchanges, of course, provide much of the dramatic force in the 1955 play *Inherit the Wind.*

J. Laurie Wallace's portrait was painted more than 20 years before the Scopes trial, but still it suggests many of the discrepancies that would define Bryan's career, including his role as a representative of social Christian issues from this region (Fig. 8). Wallace seems to have understood these discrepancies and tried to represent the tensions that followed from them. The first thing viewers notice when they look at the painting, for example, is that the eyes of the "Great Commoner" are directed at a spot just above our heads. Through this technique Wallace suggests that the popular and populist agenda Bryan advocated with such heartfelt passion was also a complex intellectual undertaking. The pairing of heart and head and the kind of dichotomies that follow are repeated elsewhere, most explicitly through the pair of books that sit upon the table. Probably allusions to Scripture or to the traditional concept of a Book of God and a Book of Nature, together these volumes both yield and hide information about a divine Kingdom. As if he was responding directly to the challenge posed by the availability and closure of the texts, Bryan faces them but keeps his body at a sharp angle to both. His hands repeat the established pattern—half-opened, half-closed—and the flowers, with their sharply contrasting colors—the passionate purple and the more innocent white—complete the picture.

In the light of the tensions Wallace depicts, it is interesting to interpret the most famous words Bryan ever uttered as expressions of social Christian rhetoric from the plains or western regions. When the Democratic party gathered in Chicago in 1896 to nominate a candidate for President, the most contested matter of the day was "the silver issue." Important to residents of the plains and western states who depended upon the value of silver to sustain economic growth, "silver" was a social Christian issue insofar as the proposed change to a gold standard seemed to many believers an unjust impediment to establishing God's Kingdom. As John Howard points out in *The Story of a Canon*, "the two metals have been linked together and used as money since the time of Abraham and Ephron." "History," he goes on to assert, "both sacred and profane attests to [this fact]."[31]

As a congressman from Nebraska, Bryan supported the two-metal standard, and the oration he delivered to the delegates won him the nomination of the party. The most quoted lines of the speech begin this way:

> Having behind us the producing masses of this nation and the world, supported by the commercial interests, the laboring interests, and the toilers everywhere, we will answer their demand for a gold standard . . . .[32]

With these words, Bryan sharpens a distinction made in the first part of this essay between eastern and western voices within the social Christian movement. The "demand for a gold standard" is made by easterners, more specifically by those who live in east-coast "cities." Earlier in the speech Bryan asserted that some

---

[31] Hill, The Story of a Canon, 236-37.

have come to the convention to "tell us that the great cities are in favor of the gold standard; we reply," he notes, "that the great cities rest upon our broad and fertile prairies." The dichotomy of an "us" and a "them" is regional. Westerners are not easterners.

What follows these opening lines are the words that won Bryan the nomination and earned his speech a place in virtually all anthologies of great American oratory. "We will answer their demand for a gold standard by saying to them: You shall not press down upon the brow of labor this crown of thorns, you shall not crucify mankind upon a cross of gold."[33] Read as expressions of a "western" social Christian rhetoric, these words gain particular meanings from their association with that region. Immanence is certainly implied within Bryan's allusion—the crucifixion can happen again in a contemporary setting—but Bryan deliberately avoids any specific references to a single, identifiable Christ figure. "Labor" receives the crown of thorns; "Mankind" is crucified. Speaking to a convention hall full of Democrats about an issue that he has already described in regional terms, Bryan refuses to identify his Christ as either Democratic or western. The result is that the God who, through Bryan's vocabulary and images, is clearly immanent, remains "other." Not all mankind are laborers; in fact, farmers on the prairies probably do not understand themselves this way. It is possible, in other words, to be a part of the convention audience, to hear Bryan's words and imagine the savior they conjure up, to apply the experience to me yet at the same time think of it all as more appropriate for someone else, for members, say, of a group to which I do not belong.

This distinction introduces a tension similar to the one identified and discussed above. The social Christian context traced in this essay enriches the notions of self and other that emerge from Bryan's imagery. And just as tension

[32] William Jennings Bryan, "The Cross of Gold," in *The World's Best Orations*, ed. David J. Brewer St. Louis: Fred P. Kaiser, 1900), vol. 2, 701.

generates irony when Nina Ellison sends her protagonist into a new land to discover the past or George Harvey wraps the town of Burlington with religious meanings by setting its church on a hill, so Bryan uses the irony that defines the passion of Christ to offer messages of warning and hope. Those who are crucified—decidedly not, says Bryan, "those who live upon the Atlantic coast, but rather the hardy pioneers who have braved all the dangers of the wilderness"—those people and their cause cannot die. Bryan's social Christian rhetoric assures his audience that, even in defeat, victory follows. This is the message of tremendous promise and creativity that repeatedly rescues western experiences of dichotomy and tension. After all, though it be made of thorns, it is still a crown one wears out on the prairie. For social Christian advocates, such is the problem—and the promise—of the west.

[33] *Ibid.*

4

CHRISTIAN SOCIALISM AND GOD'S PLOT

"Christian socialism was loosely organized, vague, individualistic, but its influence was undoubtedly large. . . . The roster of the *New Time*, edited in Chicago by B.O. Flower and Frederick Upham Adams as an unofficial Christian Socialist organ, showed how varied a group it attracted—Hamlin Garland, Edward Bellamy, and Hazen Pingree subscribed to it, Parsons, Debs, Bemis, Jerry Simpson wrote for it, and of these only Debs was a party Socialist. The average Christian Socialist was very likely someone like Ernest H. Crosby, or William Dean Howells, both of whom drew ideas from George, Jefferson, Tolstoy, Whitman, and the Bible."

Russel B. Nye, *Midwestern Progressive Politics*

If Christian socialism constitutes an entity within social Christianity, what features distinguish it from other factions in the larger movement like the more moderate Social Gospel? Others have asked similar questions. Before Nye found it to be "loosely organized" and "vague," Nicolas Paine Gilman described

Christian socialism in 1889 as "something like a society for the propagation of virtue in general." Richard T. Ely spoke of it in 1894 as motivated by "a certain spirit rather than a fixed creed." More recent critics like Paul Phillips have pointed out that "in this period socialists were as confused about what constituted socialism as Christian Socialists were about what constituted Christian Socialism."[1]

When critics and students of the period try to distinguish the movement from its counterparts they typically refer to its theology and praxis. According to these references, Christian socialism interprets key Christian symbols differently than, say, the Social Gospel. Jesus' cross, for example, does not suggest a Social Gospel theology of resurrection or the coming of God's Kingdom; rather, it

---

[1] Nicholas Paine Gilman, "Christian Socialism in America," *Unitarian Review* 32 (1889): 351; Richard T. Ely, *Socialism* (New York, 1894); Paul T.Phillips, *A Kingdom on Earth: Anglo-American Social Christianity, 1880-1940* (University Park, PA.: Pennsylvania State U. Press), 203. Despite the wisdom of Russel Nye's observation about the breadth and variety of American adherents to a Christian socialism, most students of the period have been inclined to distinguish the movement sharply from other forms of social Christianity, particularly the Social Gospel. Nye himself follows the lead of those classic histories of the period, C. Howard Hopkins' *The Rise of the Social Gospel in American Protestantism* and Henry F. May's *Protestant Churches and Industrial America*, as he delineates the elements of a larger social Christian movement into conservative, progressive, and radical branches. According to this system, certain figures are placed in distinct camps: Joseph Cook, Minot Savage, and Russell Conwell belong to the conservatives; Walter Rauschenbusch, Washington Gladden, and Richard T. Ely are progressive; William Dwight Porter Bliss and George Davis Herron are radicals. Although such groupings are useful, typically they depend upon historical schemes that base comprehensive distinctions on rather brief periods of time. In these schemes not only does "radical social Christianity" have its own "conservative," "progressive," and "radical" phases, so do the careers of its practitioners. Herron is the most frequently cited example of a prophetic voice that changes significantly with time. "As his thought matured he became more radical," wrote Hopkins and Ronald White in their widely used documentary history *The Social Gospel, Religion and Reform in Changing America*. The problem with this approach is that Hopkins and White must base their conclusions on documents that do not allow time for much "maturity" to occur. Between their example of an early work by Herron, *The Larger Christ*, and a later piece, *The New Redemption*, there are but two years (1891-1893). Moreover, when read closely the two texts reveal far more similarities than differences. Russel B. Nye, *Midwestern Progressive Politics, A Historical Study of Its Origins and Development, 1870-1950* (East Lansing: Michigan State College Press, 1951); C. Howard Hopkins, *The Rise of the Social Gospel in American Protestantism, 1865-1915* (New Haven: Yale U. Press, 1940); Henry F. May, *Protestant Churches and Industrial America* (New York: Octagon Books, 1949; 1977). Ronald C. Hopkins and C. Howard Hopkins, *The Social Gospel, Religion and Reform in a Changing America* (Philadelphia: Temple U. Press, 1976), 176.

challenges us to sacrifice for one another. According to Christian socialism, if we answer that challenge certain practical consequences follow, notable among them a deep reservation about the ability of the institutional church to prepare believers for God's Kingdom. While Social Gospel advocates seem to remain committed to a Church that they understand to be the best hope for introducing the Kingdom on earth, Christian socialists find it difficult to support any institution, sacred or profane, and maintain their commitment to a principal of sacrifice.

To clarify these arguments it is helpful to move beyond generalizations about both movements to specific examples that permit more detailed comparisons and contrasts. One place to start would be with the writings of certain key figures. Between 1894 and 1910 both George D. Herron, leading proponent of a Christian socialism, and Walter Rauschenbusch, champion of the Social Gospel, wrote separate analyses of that great social document from Matthew 6:9-13, the Lord's Prayer. Although Herron composed his as part of a series of public lectures and Rauschenbusch authored his as an occasion for personal reflection, that difference only serves to highlight their contrasting approaches to a text that both men understood as fundamental to social life. Frequently cited as representative examples of the "radical" and "progressive" elements in a larger social Christian movement, Herron and Rauschenbusch, respectively, articulate important positions when they write about the prayer. Read together, their reflections provide excellent opportunities to sharpen the distinctions between the approaches to social Christianity that they "represent."

If scholars of the period—from Hopkins, Mays, and Nye to Donald Gorrell, Susan Curtis, and Paul T. Phillips—are correct when they argue that different theological positions distinguish Herron's "radical" Christian socialism from Rauschenbusch's Social Gospel, then certain theological contrasts ought to emerge directly as the two men interpret the words of Jesus from the Gospel.[2] Indeed Herron seems to announce those differences as he begins his commentary on Matthew. "To enter the holy place of this prayer," he writes, "is to lose sight of self." As he continues, it becomes clear that a Christian Socialist theology of sacrifice is fundamental to his analysis. "Freedom," according to Herron, "is deliverance from the sphere of self-interest," and through sacrifice opportunities emerge that lead us to recognize "the oneness of men with God."[3]

Although Herron's theological foundation is explicit, it does not provide the anticipated features that would enable readers to identify a genuinely unique quality to his commentary. In fact, Rauschenbusch bases his interpretation of Matthew on a very similar theological position. In "The Social Meaning of the Lord's Prayer," Rauschenbusch writes that to follow Jesus is to outgrow "crude selfishness" and develop a "consciousness of human solidarity." Just as Herron describes a "oneness" between men and God, Rauschenbusch asserts that "we are one in our sin and our salvation."[4] Both writers, therefore, read the prayer as a means to address issues of social solidarity. Herron refers to it as a way for Christians to stimulate the "perfect and progressive society" that is the ideal of all social Christian advocates, and Rauschenbusch echoes that position when he calls it simply "part of the heritage of social Christianity,"[5]

The common theological emphasis on solidarity with one another and with God leads to a second similarity between the two commentaries: a shared suspicion of the institutional church. Herron's commitment to sacrifice results in

[2] Donald K. Gorrell, *The Age of Social Responsibility, The Social Gospel in the Progressive Era* (Macon: Mercer U. Press, 1988); Susan Curtis, *A Consuming Faith, The Social Gospel and Modern American Culture* (Baltimore: Johns Hopkins U. Press, 1991); Paul T. Phillips, *A Kingdom on Earth, Anglo-American Social Christianity, 1880-1940* (University Park: Penn State Press, 1996).

[3] George Davis Herron, "The Political Economy of the Lord's Prayer," in Herron, *The Christian Society* (Chicago Fleming H. Revel Company, 1894), 127,137.

[4] Walter Rauschenbusch, "The Social Meaning of the Lord's Prayer," in *Walter Rauschenbusch, Selected Writings*, ed. Winthrop S. Hudson (New York: Paulist Press, 1984), 212-213.

his challenge to organizations that have "have failed to fulfill the Kingdom of God in . . . society."[6] By all definitions, his words reflect the "radical" claims of Christian Socialism. But in "The Social Meaning of the Lord's Prayer," Rauschenbusch too objects to "churchly religion." Moreover, as he refers to the prayer as a "protest" for "soldiers of the Kingdom of God," his "moderate" Social Gospel rhetoric actually grows hotter than Herron's Christian Socialist discourse.[7] In the end, neither a theological explanation that begins with "solidarity" nor a more practical interpretation based on levels of distrust for the institutional church seem to provide readers with the resources they need to describe a significant difference between these writers or the movements represented by these samples of their work.

A new approach holds more promise. The terms selected by Herron and Rauschenbusch to discuss this prayer suggest that at least the "intellectual" differences between these two men may exhibit themselves more profoundly in their "literary" technique. Something as basic as the choice of words by both authors gives these essays their distinct tones, and the placement of those words indicates that the essays cohere in different ways and exhibit different styles. In these commentaries on the Lord's Prayer, literary elements precede content and actually provide readers with significant ways to recognize and distinguish the "centrist" Social Gospel theology of Rauschenbusch from the more "radical" theology of Christian socialism advanced by Herron.

Certain contrasts and incongruities are evident from the outset. Rauschenbusch begins with a collection of words and phrases that establish a singular tone and associate the prayer with the character of Jesus. Matthew 6:9-

---

[5] *Ibid.*, 212.

[6] Herron, "The Political Economy of the Lord's Prayer," 135.

[7] Rauschenbusch, "The Social Meaning of the Lord's Prayer," 211-212. Both writers even use similar metaphors from the language of health. Herron says that we pray this prayer "so that we may have moral and physical health to do God's will in human relations." Rauschenbusch says that we speak it to avoid the "diverse diseases of mammonism."

13, he writes, is "the purest expression of the mind of Jesus." It "crystallizes his thoughts." Furthermore, it not only allows us access to what Jesus is thinking, it makes "transparent" his feelings of "childlike trust" in God and "peace of the soul." In a word, Rauschenbusch starts his analysis with a keen interest in the "atmosphere" generated within the prayer for its readers.[8]

Herron begins much differently. For him the Lord's Prayer does not ask us to consider Jesus' character but rather the nexus of events that God must control in order for Jesus to be effective. Herron's vocabulary virtually ignores issues of individual character and sets a very different tone. In Herron's essay, "The Political Economy of the Lord's Prayer," Jesus' words express nothing less than God's expertise in the "science" that "regulates production and distribution" between human beings, the "system" that "provides for the economic needs of all." The same words that had revealed to Rauschenbusch "a certain spiritual nobility" in the "heart and mind of Jesus"[9] show to Herron God's ability "to regulate the economic life of man, . . . associate men in perfect harmony," and thereby institute a "divine government of the world."[10]

The words each writer uses indicates their preoccupations with different literary conventions. If the best way to describe the dominant literary element in Rauschenbusch is to call it "characterization," then one way to contrast Herron is to note his interest in "plot." For Herron what matters is the structure or order writers use to control action: "The Kingdom of God," he writes, "is a natural law" that functions to support the "regulation of production and distribution through communion with God."[11] Rauschenbusch reads "give us this day our daily bread" and claims that it speaks to a "basis of life": "the elemental need of men for bread."[12] Herron utters the same phrase but hears "a vast social obligation."[13]

---

[8] *Ibid.*, 211.
[9] *Ibid.*, 213.
[10] Herron, "The Political Economy of the Lord's Prayer," 126, 137.
[11] *Ibid.*, 137-38.
[12] Rauschenbusch, "The Social Meaning of the Lord's Prayer," 213.

As distinguished from Rauschenbusch's text, Herron's essay helps to define Christian socialism as a movement that interprets separate incidents in terms of the roles they play within larger plots. At one point in his analysis of the Lord's Prayer, for example, Herron turns to Genesis 22 and the story of Abraham and Isaac, a tale that he feels demands literary terminology to describe its "form" and understand the "language" it "speaks."[14] Part "ethical romance," part "moral adventure," part "tragedy," this "whole story turns upon the sacrifice of Isaac."[15] Herron reads the tale for its plot, concentrating on actions that build to a "climacteric" moment when God stays Abraham's hand.[16] What follows constitutes the "descending action" in which we live, a "Social Sabbath" that comprises the denouement of "God's creativity."[17]

When readers ignore this focus on plot and discuss the work of Herron and other Christian socialists as further examples of the Social Gospel emphasis on individual "character," they miss opportunities to clarify differences and establish connections with other works. Such confusion begins early in the interpretation of the social Christian movement. In 1889 Lyman Abbott, who considered himself a leader in the Social Gospel movement, wrote an essay for *The North American Review* that challenged "the methods of . . . a Christian Socialism" because, as he said, proponents of that movement misunderstand the role of "character."[18] Christian Socialists address the "character" of a single entity that Abbott calls "the social organism." They "strike at the vice in the organism; demand reform in the organism; seek changes that can be wrought by legislation in the organism."[19] Such an emphasis opposes "the way of the Christian Church" for, according to

---

[13] Herron, "The Political Economy of the Lord's Prayer," 144.
[14] *Ibid.*, 15, 16, 29, 45.
[15] *Ibid.*, 14.
[16] *Ibid.*, 23, 19.
[17] *Ibid.*, 25, 45.
[18] Lyman Abbott, "Christianity versus Socialism," *The North American Review* (April 1889), in Paul H.Boase, ed. *The Rhetoric of Christian Socialism* (New York: Random House, 1969), 68.

Abbott, in Christianity only individuals can constitute "organisms" capable of reform. "Society" does not "sin" and is not "saved."[20] In this way the "Christian Church," he continues, does not "disesteem" social reform; but it also "does not undertake to be a social reform organization." "Christ proceeded on the assumption that, if we can get rid of sin in the individual, we shall get rid of evil in the state."[21] In Abbott's analysis, the crucial difference between the Social Gospel and Christian socialism depends upon a single issue: "the reform of character."

But when Herron refers to Abraham and Isaac as "vital and sustaining members" of a "human organism," he does not introduce terms or ideas that ascribe "character" to this entity. Rather, he discusses the role of the organism within a sequence of ordered events. "These two men were sent upon a divine errand. . . . They saw a human history to be made, a human destiny to be wrought out, in which they were to be God's organs."[22] The character of the social organism is not at issue; what matters is whether it follows a "most orderly proceeding."[23] As in the "Declaration of Principles" that Herron supported when the Society of Christian Socialists released them in 1889, the term "character" is an afterthought. Both Herron's analysis of the Lord's Prayer and the more comprehensive "Declaration" shift the focus of readers away from issues of "character" and toward matters of God as "source and guide" in a "general plan" of redemption.

When the most popular periodical associated with Christian socialism, *The Kingdom*, appeared in 1894 it also disputed Abbott's notions and sought to turn readers away from a focus on character. The inaugural issue challenged those

---

[19] *Ibid.*, 69.
[20] *Ibid.*, 73.
[21] *Ibid.*, 70, 73.
[22] Herron, "The Political Economy of the Lord's Prayer," 25.
[23] *Ibid.*, 43-44.

who would "define Christianity as consisting of honesty and truth telling."[24] Rather than describe the Kingdom of God in terms that would associate it with the development of individual lives or even with a single social organism, members of its editorial board distinguished the Kingdom as a "divine order" meant to structure "the disorder of the present."[25] In an 1898 editorial, George Black praised Tennyson's "In Memoriam" as the high water mark of poetic utterance in this age because it addressed that theme "used now more than any other" to describe the Kingdom, "unity"—that organizational principle that "allows us to hear one clear harp in divers tones." In God's Kingdom the value of such unity varies, but it is most important, says Black, for a "world-truth: the truth of nations, of civilizations, institutions, laws, and religions" and only in the end for "individual character."[26]

When Christian writers, thinkers, and activists support socialism during these years it is because they can associate its principles not simply with action but with certain unified actions best described as "plotted." For example, when temperance advocate Frances Willard confesses to *The Kingdom* "I believe the things Christian socialism stands for," she gives the following reasons: "it is God's way out of the wilderness and into the Promised Land." The quote, printed on the cover of the February 24, 1898 issue, not only helps explain why Willard supported Christian socialism but also how she distinguished it from other social Christian movements. The Social Gospel sought for a nation "full of real Christian men and women, who 'deal justly, love mercy, and walk humbly with God'"; it exhorted men and women to follow Christ's "doctrine" of "fair dealing to others, as you would yourself be done by."[27] By contrast, Christian socialism introduces a reference to "planned actions" into Willard's text and requires her to

---

[24] George A. Gates, "Prospectus for *The Kingdom*," *The Kingdom* (April 20, 1894), 3.

[25] *Ibid.*, 5.

[26] George D. Black, "Editorial," *The Kingdom* (February 3, 1898): 323.

[27] Frances Willard, "The Coming Brotherhood," *Arena* (August 1892), in Boase, *The Rhetoric of Christian Socialism*, 85.

attend to the basic sequence of events in a story. The Social Gospel applies the words of Jesus to individual lives; Willard implies that Christian socialism asks believers to locate those lives within a divine plot that, like all great plots, is both very familiar and strikingly new.

According to Herron, Jesus himself enters into such a plot, appearing "on the scene" when John the Baptist "was in the noontide of his popularity." This plot limits Jesus' growth until the story of the Baptist "rises up in the magnificence of its unselfishness," climaxes, and orchestrates the action so that John "vanishes from the scene." "The lessening of John was the enlargement of the Christ," writes Herron as he describes the ascending and descending action of both tales.[28] God's plot appears in "the book which only the slain Lamb is worthy to open," a text written by God, author of "the sign" that audiences too often "misread and hate."[29]

The Christian socialism espoused by a prolific writer like Herron and a well-organized group such as the Society of Christian Socialists is explicit about the proper human response to God's work. All true Christians also are socialists, and as such all must allow God to inscribe their lives into his plot. "Our work," writes Herron, "is not to construct, but to make way for God's construction."[30] We "hallow God's name by making our life a word of God"[31] that God speaks, according to Herron, within "the drama" that is "the history of man."[32] Frances Willard concurs, pointing out that, as Christian socialists, we must strive to becomes texts within a plot that moves us all from wilderness to the promised land. In this we become "living Bibles, in which our fellowmen may read [God's] will . . . words of God made flesh."[33]

---

[28] George D. Herron, *The Larger Christ* (Chicago: Fleming H. Revel, 1891), 75-77.

[29] George D. Herron, *The New Redemption* (New York: Thomas Y. Crowell, 1893), 123, 44.

[30] George D. Herron, "Letter," *The Kingdom* (April, 1894): 5.

[31] Herron, "The Political Economy of the Lord's Prayer," 130.

[32] Herron, *The Christian Society*, 55.

[33] *Ibid.*, 154.

In 1889 Christian socialists advertised and promoted with great zeal a novel that dramatized the way individual characters become "one" with God's texts. When James MacArthur reviewed *Metzerott, Shoemaker* for W.D.P. Bliss's *The Dawn* he called it "splendid" and insisted that, in its author Katherine Pearson Woods, "Christian Socialism has found *par excellence* its novelist."[34] In Louis Metzerott, Woods had created a character whose identity was bound up with Scripture, not as a symbolic Christ figure but as one who tries to write himself into the Gospel plot.

The book takes its title from its central character, Karl Metzerott, a shoemaker from the poor quarter of Micklegard, whose wife Dora dies, leaving him alone to raise their only son, Louis. At odds with the local pastor and embittered by his wife's death, Karl becomes an atheist who advocates socialism and prophesies the coming "commune." Louis is exposed to Christianity through the influence of two female boarders Karl originally takes in while his wife is alive, Sally and Susan Price. He allows both to remain in his home after his wife dies.

The boy learns to read by studying words in the Bible and then enacting the plots of Biblical tales, and this early experience is crucial to the way he develops. Increasingly, Louis takes his identity from Scripture stories he hears, reads, and eventually imitates. For example, as a child he looks at the letters in the gospel and decides to refashion the story they tell by building the words out of wooden blocks. But in order to understand those words he actually "divides" their letters like loaves and fishes with the boy he plays with, a cripple named Freddy.[35] He goes on to learn words from the Book of Isaiah and then discovers them again as he reads to Freddy "'bout the Christ child."[36] He gains insight into Jesus'

---

[34] James MacArthur, "A Christian Socialist in Fiction" *The Dawn* (August 1889), 3

[35] Katherine Pearson Woods, *Metzerott, Shoemaker* (New York: Thomas Y. Crowell, 1889), 137.

[36] *Ibid.*, 136.

character by grasping the synopses of plots in "a picture Bible."[37] He plays Abraham to Freddy's Isaac, and as his friend sits "alone in the room impersonating ten lepers," Louis commands him to "arise and walk." [38]

"You're a real little Christ-child yourself," Susan Price says fondly to Louis. Eventually the plot identifies Louis in this manner as well.[39] By the end of the novel Woods sacrifices Louis so that others, particularly Karl Metzerott, the shoemaker, will believe, and in a final scene we learn that the children who gather around an old Karl Metzerott to hear his stories "become at times confused" about the deeds of Jesus and Louis: they can't tell which one "'vided the tin soldiers" with his playmates and invited neighbors to "share his dinner of soup."[40] Karl Metzerott's early admonition that his son "be a little Christ-kind" comes true, and when it does readers find that the plot unites the two dominant elements in the book, Christianity and socialism.[41]

A somewhat more intriguing use of "texts" as symbols or motives for emplotted actions comes in a second novel, Albion Tourgee's 1889 effort, *Murvale Eastman, Christian Socialist*.[42] This book tells a complicated and convoluted tale of a young Christian minister named Murvale Eastman, who tries to fulfill his role as pastor to a wealthy parish while also dating the daughter of the richest parishioner and working extra hours as a streetcar driver both to help end a local strike and to assist an injured driver. Although the book is much less focused than Woods's and by no means as successful, it nevertheless parallels *Metzerrott, Shoemaker* in important ways. Both novels depict various late nineteenth-century social classes in contact across an urban center. Both introduce religious themes through the figure of a minister but deepen those

[37] *Ibid.*, 138.
[38] *Ibid.*, 141.
[39] *Ibid.*, 136.
[40] *Ibid.*, 373.
[41] *Ibid.*, 97.
[42] Albion Tourgee, *Murvale Eastman, Christian Socialist* (New York: Fords, Howard, & Hulbert, 1889).

themes with other characters who have little use for organized religion. Both depend upon the permutations of plot, not the development of character, to attract and keep readers.

Both also use secondary characters to great advantage as they dramatize action. The counterpart to Louis Metzerott is an injured streetcar driver named Jonas Underwood, who opens the story as he convalesces from injuries he suffered while operating his car as a scab driver during a labor strike. Laid out on a cot in Murvale Eastman's office, Jonas is unable to move because every time he tries violent coughing ensues and causes his lungs to hemorrhage. A local physician refers to his episodes as "paroxysms" and notes that this most recent attack began while Jonas and his wife ate a picnic at a town park directly across from Murvale Eastman's parish. Jonas's collapse from one of these fits keeps his character in a single position for the entire novel and severely limits his ability to change or develop. However, despite his limited opportunity to grow, he plays a crucial role. In the end virtually all incidents in the novel run through Jonas, and as a figure who connects present and past actions, he constitutes a motivating force.

Although his doctor assumes that the "paroxyms" began with this most recent incident, Jonas knows that their origins are neither the picnic nor even the attack on his cab months earlier. A veteran of the Civil War, Jonas has carried within his lung a lead bullet that the accident with his cab simply aggravated. His fall in the park actually dislodged the bullet. With a trembling hand and an enormous sense of relief, Jonas presents the flattened piece of lead to the doctor in a bloody handkerchief. The doctor receives it with much skepticism, for no one has believed Jonas's account of the wound, especially the government, which has refused to recognize him in writing for a "sense of duty performed."[43]

[43] Albion Tourgee, *Murvale Eastman, Christian Socialist*, 23.

Recognition comes in the form of a letter only after Jonas has rid himself of the bullet. Tourgee is careful to depict this award as an exchange of texts, for the letter is one text and the bullet another. As the doctor points out while examining the bloody slug with Murvale, "at the upper part of that hollow cone were always stamped in the enemy's ammunition the letters C.S., surrounded by a little ring." Significantly, on this bullet the ring that binds these signs of the Confederate States is worn away. Despite its wear, however, the doctor asserts that the "piece of lead tells . . . a wonderful story. Those letters which you can distinguish are the trade-mark of a buried nation." Together they are, as the action shows, a text that Tourgee knows must be erased or purged if the plot of *Murvale Eastman* and its 1889 setting are to seem credible.[44]

In his Preface to the novel Tourgee announces a conviction that helps explain this historical reference to the war: "The thought of yesterday," he writes, "fixes the tendency of to-day." "During the last half-century," Tourgee continues, post-Civil War thinking had been dominated by the urge to consolidate: the "segregation of capital in a few hands," he maintains "has been equaled only by the restriction of opportunity." As a result of this drive toward consolidation, "the most tremendous forces have moved with unprecedented energy toward the subjection of the individual."[45] The presence and power of such forces constitute a "background" against which authors are able "to trace certain characters."[46] Tourgee conceives of his characters quite deliberately as "texts" and represents them to his readers as passages in his story. The function of both Jonas

[44] *Ibid.*, 106. Tourgee would have been very familiar with the subject. Wounded twice during the Civil War, he settled in the south as a carpetbagger from Ohio who eventually sat as a judge on the Superior Court of North Carolina. He also was aware of how a single letter could provide a potent trademark. To advocate a number of political reforms in the state he published anonymously a collection of letters that came to be known by the mark Tourgee signed, "C." The unpopular positions Tourgee assumed, including his scathing expose of the Ku Klux Klan entitled *The Invisible Empire*, prompted several attempts on his life.

[45] *Ibid.*, i.

[46] *Ibid.*, v.

Underwood and Murvale Eastman is that they operate within Tourgee's plot as "sites" where important pieces of writing interact and respond to one another.

When Jonas, for example, physically rejects the symbolic markings of a past war, he proceeds to receive not one but two other texts: his letter of recognition from the government and a mysterious opal amulet that had belonged to his long-lost daughter. Engraved with the letters DXV, the amulet had been on his daughter's neck when she disappeared mysteriously twenty years earlier. Now reunited with Jonas, this "text" connects two additional characters (Jonas's daughter and her guardian) to the central plot and eventually explains their association with Murvale Eastman. Moreover, the arrival of the amulet alerts Jonas to his daughter's presence; like the bullet he coughs from his lung, the opal and all it represents is a part of him. Murvale misreads its inscription, thinking it is an ancient Latin abbreviation for "Christ, the Son of God," and he speculates that the stone "may date back to the Catacombs."[47] Jonas recognizes the stone as something much more personal, and he interprets it correctly as the initials of his grandfather, Daniel Xemines Valentine.[48]

Tourgee's decision to balance in Jonas the loss of one text with the arrival of another extends the images of symmetrical arrangement that open the book. "Inheritance and environment" are the two words that Tourgee chooses to begin his Preface to the novel, a document in which he tries to prepare readers for the sense of equilibrium or symmetry—what Tourgee calls in Chapter XLI a "duplex nature"—that follows. Throughout the preface Tourgee juxtaposes in single sentences words that suggest balance: "yesterday" and "today," "self-government" and "impulse for control," "segregation and opportunity," "high and low," "the

---

[47] *Ibid.*, 303.

[48] Both readings of the stone emphasize its ability to fill dual roles. For Jonas of course it represents both the presence and absence of the child who disappeared while wearing it. For Murvale the stone, which is shaped like a fish, originally served both to hide and to reveal its original wearer. "Intended to be a confession of faith which might avouch for the bearer to other believers," the symbolic communication of the amulet prevented it from "betraying [early Christians] to their enemies. *Ibid.*, 303.

many and the few," "personal independence" and "social forces." He even concludes the preface with a quote from Matthew Arnold that introduces the novel as only "half a truth" to which the reader evidently adds the full complement.[49]

The quality of "balance" that Tourgee gives to Jonas finds additional expression in Murvale Eastman, a second character functioning as a "site" for the negotiation of texts. The one individual who is able to "fold away" in his mind thoughts of his fiancée after she leaves him, "turn down the brightest page in his memory" and go out to preach God's ordinances "written in heart and soul, in brain and fiber, as well as . . .on tables of stone," Murvale is associated throughout the novel with written works.[50] His sermons on Christian socialism define his role as protagonist and make him integral to the plot. Reported "verbatim" in the local newspaper, those sermons lead to his broken engagement with Lillian Kishu and to his role as an agent of change in the community. Insofar as the press promotes his position as a Christian Socialist, they do so by reporting his words. As a result, Murvale continues his role as a text within the novel, "'good' for a column in any paper of the city and from a quarter to a half column in the great dailies of other cities. . . ."[51]

When Murvale Eastman preaches to his congregation in the early chapters of the book he stands before them with a "crumpled letter" in one hand. Written by a parishioner who calls for the poor to be content with their lot, the letter functions for Murvale like Jonas's amulet, as a text designed to motivate action. Murvale's response to the letter is to preach as a Christian socialist, calling upon "capital" and "Labor" to resolve their problems and justifying his charge with still another document, the scripture reading for the day, 2 Sam.12:1. That passage begins with the words "There were two men in one city—the same city . . . the one rich and the other poor" and, as Nathan's parable to King David, it is ideal for

---

[49] *Ibid.*, 1-6.
[50] *Ibid.*, 242-43, 265.
[51] *Ibid.*, 130.

a long disquisition on character development and transformation.[52] Yet Murvale uses it as George Herron would: as an opportunity to discuss God's plan for us. "'This sentence is an epitome of history,'" he says. "'Designed for a particular case, it is yet a universal truth.'"[53] Herron's claim that "a man must live, as the old German mystics used to say, as though he himself were God," actually presumes Murvale Eastman's most basic insight here as he delivers his sermon: that we act as part of "the great Passion Play of life."[54]

The same year that Herron published his analysis of the Lord's Prayer in *The Christian Society*, and just five years after Tourgee wrote *Murvale Eastman, Christian Socialist*, Archibald McCowan published a little-known novel titled *Christ, the Socialist*.[55] The story revolves around the friendship of two men, Reverend David Burkley, pastor of the First Presbyterian Church of Springford Connecticut, and Robert Stewart, principal of the village school, whose abstract arguments about Christian socialism become quite real as workers at a local mill decide to strike. The novel is weak throughout; long monologues either support or oppose Christian socialism and fill most of the pages. The action builds to Burkley's accidental death, which serves as a sacrifice to end the strike and a climax to the tale.

After Burkley's death, however, the narrator indicates that some of the pastor's friends discover two "texts" hidden in a "pigeon hole" in his desk. These writings continue the arguments between Burkley and Stewart but at a different level. The first, written by Burkley, the minister, expounds his opposition to Christian socialism. The second comes from Stewart and, unlike his previous arguments, this one imaginatively describes a dream he has had. In this dream Jesus appears to a large crowd in the midst of Springford where he stands to

---

[52] *Ibid.*, 53.

[53] *Ibid.*

[54] Herron, "The Political Economy of the Lord's Prayer," 130-31; Tourgee, *Murvale Eastman*, 44.

[55] Archibald McCowan, *Christ, the Socialist* (Boston: Arena Publishing, 1894).

castigate almost everyone who holds a prominent social position, from "rings and bosses" to "lawyers" to "rich men," "corporations," and "journalists." He calls for them to "turn ye from your unbelief; cast aside your errors, embrace the truth, follow the path of justice and righteousness." If they succeed, "even [they] shall be forgiven."[56]

By no means convincing, the scene nevertheless is a remarkable example of the way art and theology serve the concept of plot in works dedicated to a Christian socialist message. Herron, Woods, and Tourgee all allowed their belief in God's "plot" for creation to guide the ways they represent human character and action. McCowan goes even further, eschewing all pretense to character development and giving the reader a figure of Jesus who simply proclaims the emplotted fate of all humankind. McCowan seems to answer Herron's call for men to "love like God" as he places Jesus in the city and silences all other voices, even all other noises. "And lo a miracle was being performed: cars and wagons passed up and down the streets on both sides of the park, and still the life of a busy city went on as usual, but not a sound came to distract the attention of the audience."[57] In Herron, Woods, and Tourgee characters had been described as texts and then made to follow the ascending and descending action of a fixed plot. Here God "himself" follows this pattern and, as a text, is literally "pigeon-holed" within the author's writing desk.

The restrictive setting diminishes the artistic quality of the story and also illustrates the limitations of Christian socialism from this period. The strong emphasis upon purposeful and sequential actions in this body of literature frequently threatens to weaken the importance of events that comprise the very plots its champions. As some proponents of a broader, more comprehensive social Christian message realized, the significance of a divine "plot" depended upon the fact that creation, fall, and redemption still happen to individual

[56] *Ibid.*, 350-51.

believers. Their quest for a more suitable vocabulary to express the interaction of social need and individual redemption led many to turn to the concepts of "person" and "personality," two notions that, as later "personalist" philosophers would argue, had the potential to fuse individuals with their actions, characters and their plots.[58]

---

[57] Ibid., 346.

[58] For an interpretation of personalist philosophy see Thomas O. Buford, "Personalism and Education: A Philosophical Retrospect/Prospect." *Proceedings of the Twentieth World Congress of Philosophy* (1998). *The Paideia Project* at www.bu.edu/wcp/Papers/Educ/EducBufo.

Frank Beard, *As Conscience Paints Him*

From Fifty Great Cartoons (Chicago: The Ram's Horn Press, 1899)
There are days in everybody's life when he sits alone with his conscience. The world and its undeserved blame or praise is shut out of that silent chamber. With his truthful guest the man of rags and the man of millions, the woman of toil and the woman of ease, must hold weekly if not daily and hourly communion. At these times the picture of the real self is thrown upon the vivid background of years. Now the false-hearted or boastful or proud will see and hear admonitions that would not be brooked from preacher or friend. True character divested of conventional habiliments of conduct through which the eyes of men cannot peer, will stand bleak, ragged and forlorn. "Paint me as I am," cried Cromwell, in righteous rage when the artist began to paint out of his portrait a slight disfigurement of his face. This he did though he knew that his portrait would go down through generations and thus perpetuate his ungainly visage. Who of us can say to conscience, "Paint me as I am though the world sees and the future sees me, let not my real self be hidden!

"Their conscience also bearing witness, and their thoughts the meanwhile accusing or else excusing one another." Romans 2:15.

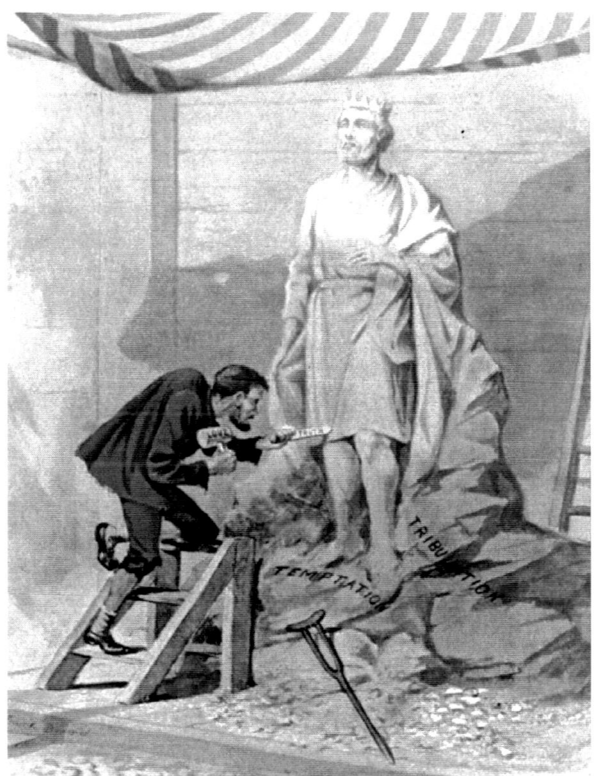

Frank Beard, *His Real Self,* From *Fifty Great Cartoons* (Chicago: The Ram's Horn Press, 1899)

Every man has two natures. Under the influence of one he descends to the carnal and the base, under the influence of the other he ascends to the spiritual and the noble. It is within the power of any man to pursue the former or the latter. To assist his in achieving the latter he is offered a model or pattern by which he may work. With this pattern in his eye, any one, however misshapen in mind or heart, may work out for himself a moral image, grand, perfect and enduring. In the person of Christ, God has shown us what a man ought to be, and he will never be satisfied until we approach that ideal.

"Till we all come in the unity of the faith, and of the knowledge of the Son of God, unto a perfect man, unto the measure of the stature of the fullness of Christ." *Ephesians* 4:13.

Olof Grafström, View of Portland, Oregon (1890)
The Fine Arts Museums of San Francisco, Museum Collection

Joseph Hitchens, ***Admission of Colorado to the Union*** **or** ***Jerome Chaffee Introduces Miss Columbia to Miss Colorado*** **(1884)**
Colorado Historical Society, Denver.

George Harvey, *View of Burlington* (1892)
Burlington Public Library, Burlington, IA

North Dakota Magazine 1 (May, 1906)

HEBJORN GAUSTA, *THE LAY PREACHER* (1884)
VESTERHEIM, NORWEGIAN-AMERICAN MUSEUM, DECORAH, IOWA

J. Laurie Wallace, *William Jennings Bryan* (1902), Nebraska State Historical Society, Lincoln

5

THE PERSON IN SOCIAL CHRISTIAN LITERATURE

"The PERSON Jesus Christ is the whole of Christianity."

George A. Gates, Baccalaureate Sermon, Iowa College, June 23, 1889

Within the diverse and confusing rhetoric of social Christianity, the "personalism" expressed by Gates is surprisingly direct. It generates metaphors that influence every ideological position within the larger movement: from conservative preacher Joseph Cook, who warned that unless Christians responded to poverty and unfair practices "Labor" would be "crowned king" even as "it wades knee-deep in blood";[1] to the more moderate Lyman Abbott who, despite his distrust of references to social "character," nevertheless referred to the "social

---

[1] Joseph Cook, *Boston Monday Lectures: Labor, with Preludes on Current Events* (Boston: Houghton Mifflin, 1880), reprinted in Paul H. Boase, *The Rhetoric of Christian Socialism* (New York: Random House, 1969), 42.

organism" and personified it through descriptions of its "growth," "clothing," and even its individual identity in the Parable of the Good Samaritan;[2] to W. D. P. Bliss, who helped to locate its images firmly in social Christian discourse by insisting that, like human beings, "civilization" was "created by the Divine Hand" and has given rise to a Church that can "push" for those social reforms "she" believes will lead to a "fraternal" social order.[3]

Walter Rauschenbusch sought to establish a theological basis for this social Christian model and method as late as 1917. For Rauschenbusch, St. Paul provided "the first and classical discussion in Christian thought of the nature and functioning of a composite spiritual organism." Prior to Paul were the "Old Testament prophets who saw their nation as a gigantic personality which sinned, suffered, and repented." Subsequent to Paul's message, the Church has always "claimed a continuous and enduring life of its own" as nothing less than the "body of Christ."[4]

As Ralph Luker recently has argued, a substantial though diverse group of social Christian writers precede Rauschenbusch on this point. Luker demonstrates that, before Rauschenbusch constructed his 1917 theology of the church as a "collective personality" subject to sin and redemption, numerous social Christian writers had prepared his audience. As early as 1885, for example, a "theological personalism" emerged from the metaphors social Christians used to describe different organizations. Moreover, that same sense of "personalism" controlled their prescribed "solutions" to social problems. Writers, preachers, theologians, and social critics insisted that the most profound social changes occurred when

---

[2] Lyman Abbott, "Christianity versus Socialism," *The North American Review* CXLVIII (April 1889): 447-453, reprinted in Boase, *The Rhetoric of Christian Socialism*, 70, 71,75.

[3] William Dwight Porter Bliss, editorial in *The Dawn* (May15, 1889), reprinted in Boase, *The Rhetoric of Christian Socialism*, 64-65.

[4] Walter Rauschenbusch, *Theology of the Social Gospel* (New York: Macmillan, 1917), 69-70.

Christians imagined organizations as "'persons'" condemned or redeemed by God according to New Testament principles.[5]

One important result of such imaginative acts is that, as Gates said, even those who seek to "get at" the "spirit itself" must do so through the senses.[6] Critics typically have attributed social Christian interest in the human senses to their persistent advocacy of theological immanence. In addition to Washington Gladden's statement that Jesus is "more, but not other," writers from the period provide a great deal of evidence for this claim. In 1905 Charles Cuthbert Hall, President of Union Theological Seminary in New York, insisted that "the significance of God's immanence has appeared to this generation as to none of its predecessors."[7] According to Hall, one consequence of this appearance, is that "all human life is invested with immediate importance and value." "Salvation by self-immersion in the life of the world," writes Hall, " has become the chief incentive of the Christian."[8]

Even though Hall goes on to insist that the way to "self-immersion" is through the world of sense experience where "nothing is common or unclean," students of the social Christian movement either have ignored altogether its frequent references to the body or neglected the context in which those references appear. Like William Hutchison, they have tended to interpret "immanentism" as one of a "cluster of beliefs" that include the "adaptation of religious ideas to modern culture" and "a religious-based progressivism." Once "clustered" with notions of cultural adaptation and social progressivism, immanentism becomes one more example of a social Christian commitment to the Kingdom of God as the primary aim toward which culture advances. Subsequent correlations by other

---

[5] Ralph E. Luker, *The Social Gospel in Black and White: American Racial Reform, 1885-1912* (Chapel Hill: U. of North Carolina Press, 1991), 6.

[6] *Ibid.*, 5.

[7] Charles Cuthbert Hall, *The Universal Elements of the Christian Religion* (New York: Fleming H. Revell, 1905), 271.

[8] *Ibid.*, 270-71.

scholars between the social Christian quest for the Kingdom and late nineteenth-century progressive political agendas have furthered this emphasis.

But when a church historian like Donald Gorrell isolates the claim by Walter Rauschenbusch that "the social gospel was concerned about 'a progressive social incarnation of God,'" his interpretation neglects an important context for Rauschenbush's statement.[9] The central word in this quote is "social," and Rauschenbusch uses it to join two other terms in the sentence: "progressive" and "incarnation of God." Gorrell, who is perhaps the most recent historian to examine the social Gospel in its denominational setting, tends to emphasize the relationship between the terms "social" and "progressive," thereby focusing attention on the "close interaction of social Christianity and Progressive reform."[10] Read this way, Rauchenbusch's quote seems to stress the public, political motives behind social Christian discourse.

The context for this quote, however, suggests a different interpretation. The passage comes from Chapter Fourteen of Rauschenbusch's *Theology*, and it is surrounded by references to the individual figure of Christ. The "problem of the social gospel," writes Rauschenbusch immediately before the quote, "is how the divine life of Christ can get control of human society."[11] Moreover, he follows the passage with a plea for a "Christ who is truly personal." "Just as the human race, when it appears in theology, is an amorphous metaphysical conception which could be more briefly designated by an algebraic symbol," in the same way the personality of Jesus is not allowed to be real under theological influence. According to Rauschenbusch, Jesus can no longer be "made part of a scheme of

[9] Donald Gorrell, *The Age of Social Responsibility: The Social Gospel in the Progressive Era 1900-1920* (Macon: Mercer U. Press, 1988), 269.

[10] *Ibid.*, 341. See also Aaron Abell, *The Urban Impact on American Protestantism, 1865-1900* (Cambridge: Harvard U. Press, 1943).

[11] Walter Rauschenbusch, *A Theology for the Social Gospel* (New York: Macmillan Co., 1917), 148.

salvation, the second premise in a great syllogism." For that reason the "social gospel wants to see [in Jesus] a personality able to win hearts . . . ."[12]

In this context, Rauschenbusch appears to be searching for words that will allow him to use the drama of the incarnation to describe and delineate an idea of "social" reality. Other social Christians from the period share his search. For many, to comprehend the life of an organization like the church means that one must imagine Jesus as a well-developed "character," complete with dramatic motives and all of the traits that constitute a "personality." Several important social Christian novels emphasize just this point. Recall the refrain "What Would Jesus Do?" that echoes throughout Charles Sheldon's monumental best-seller. *From Heaven to New York* is the title of Isaac George Reed's early work from 1875. *If Christ Came to Chicago* is what William T. Stead called his trend-setting 1894 novel. Edward Everett Hale answered Stead in 1895 with *If Jesus Came to Boston*. To a great extent, all of these authors constructed their novels around the imaginative acts of Jesus, the "character."[13]

As social Christian novelists discover, a question such as "What Would Jesus Do?" makes narrative sense only if readers can correlate the "bodily" experiences of both the characters in the novel and the figure of Jesus.[14] Because dramatic encounters between Jesus and other characters emphasize the physical consequences of God's incarnation, readers come to appreciate what George Gates insisted: that truth "needs to be made alive, incarnated in a person, before it has the power to do its work."[15]

[12] *Ibid.*, 148-49.

[13] Isaac George Reed, *From Heaven to New York* (New York: Optimus Printing Co., 1894; first published 1875); William T. Stead, *If Christ Came to Chicago* (Chicago: Laird and Lee, 1894); Edward Everett Hale, *If Jesus Came to Boston* (Boston: Lamson, Wolffe, 1895).

[14] Sheldon uses the grammatical form of a question to suggest the problems of such a correlation. Is Jesus really "present" in his body?

[15] Gates, "Baccalaureate Address," 5. Clearly social Christian novelists could "dramatize some social evil and then propose a solution" in ways that theologians of the movement could not; on this point see Robert Glenn Wright, *The Social Christian Novel* (Westport, CT: Greenwood Press, 1989), chapter 1. "The books of Mr. Charles M. Sheldon," wrote Walter Rauschenbuch,

According to Gates, only someone who is "fully alive" to "touch and eyes and ears" is able to connect "truth and power," potency and act.[16] His description of the human person is significant for at least two reasons. In the first place, it challenges those recent critics of the period who insist that social structures and organizations define and manipulate individuals in ways that render them powerless. According to numerous social Christian writers, the social order does not necessarily define individual lives; individuals also delineate society by establishing social parameters. From this principle it follows that a person can impose herself or himself upon society and in fact change it. Such a notion contradicts directly the theses of recent literary critics and cultural historians like June Howard and Philip Fisher, who assert that a kind of "paralysis haunts the frontier between . . . self and other" during late nineteenth-century America[17]

In the second place, Gates's description provides a long neglected context for understanding the role of vision in the culture and period, a context that recent interpretations have neglected entirely. Gates's reference to "eyes" suggests that, in a religious setting at least, "seeing" may not incapacitate viewers, diminish volition, or further an undiscriminating complicity between the self and society.

"set forth [the thought of following Jesus] with winning spirit." Moreover, as Rauschenbusch recognized, readers of this fiction discovered in it not only a winning "spirit" but also considerable physical detail. Thoughts of following Jesus, Rauschenbusch pointed out, found tangible expression in the actions of "thousands of young people trying for a week to live as Jesus would." In this manner, many readers were able to use the didactic qualities of this literature to integrate different facets and vocabularies of the social Christian message. Walter Rauschenbusch, *Christianizing the Social Order* (New York: Macmillan, 1913), 46.

[16] Gates, "Baccalaureate Address," 5.

[17] June Howard, *Form and History in American Literary Naturalism*, (Chapel Hill: U. of North Carolina Press, 1985), 111. Philip Fisher, "Acting, Reading Fortune's Wheel: *Sister Carrie* and the Life History of Objects," *American Literary Realism: New Essays*, Eric J. Sundquist, ed. (Baltimore: Johns Hopkins U. Press): 259-77; "Appearing and Disappearing in Public: Social Space in Late Nineteenth-Century American Culture," Harvard English Series, *Reconstructing American Literary History*, Sacvan Bercovitch, ed. (Cambridge: Harvard U. Press, 1986): 155-88. Although these writers concentrate on literary "realism" and "naturalism," they use both "genre" as means for making larger claims about United States culture during the period. For example, Howard argues that naturalism "does not provide a window into reality. Rather," she claims, "it reveals history indirectly in revealing itself. . ." (29). Her debt to George Lukacs is evident

Rather, it may in fact be a means to change. For Gates, the "eyes" are but one sense; we are "alive" through "touch" and "ears" as well, and there is no reason to think that he would not be willing to extend his list to include other senses that together comprise a human person. As he goes on to say, truth became human so that we could "feel the touch of the vital personality."[18]

When contemporary critics neglect to relate metaphors of visual experience to other terms that describe the senses, they ignore this important concept of "personality" as it recurs throughout this cultural record. One result of their omission is that the rhetoric of social reform loses its power to persuade. If we understand our individual relationship to the social order as one of viewer to spectacle, we are left without a critical "perspective." Reduced to "commodities," the elements of daily life become "spectacles" that motivate "viewers" by stimulating and validating their desire. Consequently, we lose the means to think against cultural trends.[19]

But if "eyes" "ears" and "touch" are terms intended to describe a fully developed "personality," and if the social order seems to possess a corresponding set of personal traits that contribute both to its "fall" and its "redemption," then the exchange between these two perhaps is not as one-sided as some have argued. Rauschenbusch's writings indicate that it is not. When first anthologized in 1950 they presented to readers a variety of topics that explored the central claim for a social personality. To save a "nation" from its "collective sins," and thereby halt

---

throughout her study, especially in her critical position that literature, "through artistic form," does "reconstitute historical reality" (24).

[18] Gates, "Baccalaureate Address," 5.

[19] The consensus of scholars of the period such as Howard, Fisher, Rachel Bowlby, and Amy Kaplan is that when "society" manipulates desire in this way it actually defines its constituents. Moreover, most maintain that the vocabulary that enables society to dominate individual members in this way comes from the lexicon of visual experience. Such "spectacles" are "other" by definition, they insist, and in the late nineteenth and early twentieth-century Americans desired otherness primarily through their eyes. On this point see especially Howard, *Form and History in American Literary Naturalism*; Fisher, "Acting, Reading Fortune's Wheel"; Rachel Bowlby, *Just Looking: Consumer Culture in Dreiser, Gissing, and Zola* (New York:

the "slow process of strangulation and asphyxiation" that threatens its "soul," these excerpts emphasized the need "of the social body . . .[to] be filled with a fresh flow of blood." According to Rauschenbusch, "a regenerate nation will look with eyes of youth across the fields of the future."[20] By contrast, those societies without the proper "field of vision" cannot "see the oncoming of the great day of God . . . ."[21]

For this 1950 anthology the editor, Benjamin Mays, President of Morehouse College, selected excerpts from a variety of Rauschenbusch's writings, including *Christianity and Social Crisis*, *Christianizing the Social Order*, and *A Theology* of *the Social Gospel* (others included *Prayers of the Social Awakening*, *The Social Principles of Jesus*, *Unto Me*, and *The New Evangelism*). The selections emphasized certain elements of Rauschenbusch's theology, most prominently his theological personalism. *A Gospel for the Social Awakening: Selections from the Writings of Walter Rauschenbusch* begins by personifying a nation that, in its "adolescence," "consumes," suffers "paralysis," and risks inviting the "worm of death" into its "heart." It ends with his prayer for a "nation . . . at strife with its own soul and . . . sinning."[22] Between this beginning and end May represents a Rauschenbusch who explores the consequences of his personalism for traditional theological categories: in May's anthology Rauschenbusch argues that "sin is transmitted along the lines of social traditions," and therefore "professions and organizations" must act as "composite personalities" who seek both "repentance and conversion."[23]

Mays' work as editor testifies not only to the prevalence of this theological personalism throughout the Rauschenbusch corpus but also to its singular

Methuen, 1985); Amy Kaplan, *The Social Construction of American Realism* (Chicago: U. Chicago Press, 1988).

[20] Benjamin E. Mays ed., *A Gospel for the Social Awakening, Selections from the Writings of Walter Rauschenbusch* (New York: Association Press, 1950), 32, 179, 29.

[21] *Ibid.*, 31, 179.

[22] *Ibid.*, 179.

[23] *Ibid.*, 92, 111.

importance for social reform in the twentieth century, particularly in the areas of racial equality and civil rights. Mays' next book, *The Negro's God as Reflected in His Literature*, chronicles the African-American response to the social, economic, and the political privileges of others. In it he suggests that the struggles of "Negroes" to overcome perceptions of themselves as "inferior people" results in their own collective "personality," which leads them to associate their character and destiny with those belonging to the Hebrews. African Americans grew "accustomed to interpret Negro slavery in terms of Egyptian bondage," and what follows their acquiescence is the hope that "as freedom came to the Hebrews it would come to the Negro."[24]

Although May develops Rauschenbusch's personalism and applies it to his analysis of African-American "ideas" of God, the task of employing this rhetoric to further civil rights falls to May's most famous student, Martin Luther King. Indeed, no less a social reformer than King conceived of the American encounter between self and society this way.[25] According to King, the "eloquent and unequivocal language" of the Declaration of Independence established as the basis for all such encounters "the dignity and the worth of human personality."[26] Because he maintained that fundamental principle, King could diagnose America as a nation with a "schizophrenic personality," one that resisted its charge to become "spiritually one." It even failed, he claimed, to commit to the physical need for a "geographical oneness." Without this respect for an integrated

---

[24] Benjamin E. Mays, *The Negro's God as Reflected in His Literature* (New York: Russell and Russell, 1938), 15, 18, 28.

[25] Ralph Luker claims that the tradition of theological personalism constituted "the most significant formal theological influence upon Martin Luther King Jr.'s intellectual development," and he calls King "the last of the great theological personalists." Ralph E. Luker, "Interpreting the Social Gospel: Reflections on Two Generations of Historiography" in Christopher H. Evans, *Perspectives on the Social Gospel: Papers from the Inaugural Social Gospel Conference at Colgate Rochester Divinity School* (Lewiston: Edwin Mellen Press, 1999), 7,9.

[26] Martin Luther King, Jr., "The American Dream," in James M. Washington, ed., *A Testament of Hope, The Essential Writings of Martin Luther King, Jr.* (San Francisco, Harper and Row, 1986), 208.

personality, the United States surrendered the vocabulary that bound it to the call for personal and holistic social reform as found in the New Testament.

"The Gospel at its best deals with the whole man," wrote King, "not only his soul but his body. . . ."[27] This interpretation of Scripture, which prompts not only King's choice of words but also his acts of resistance and commitment to reform, follows directly in his essay from the admission that, "in the early fifties I read Rauschenbusch's *Christianity and the Social Crisis*, a book which left an indelible imprint on my thinking."[28] Although he criticizes Rauschenbusch for his participation in the nineteenth-century "cult of progress," he goes on to praise him for the "sense of social responsibility" he gave to American Protestantism; a sense it "should never lose." In an effort perhaps to demonstrate his debt to social Christian patterns of thinking, King chooses to credit Rauschenbusch with a gift that involves the "sense" of a social personality, one that must "await burial" if it cannot deal with the threats to individuals that come from "social conditions" able both to "strangle" and "cripple."[29]

Like recent cultural critics, King warns his audience against placing too much faith in the rhetoric of visual experience. "I call upon you not to be detached spectators, but involved participants, in the great drama . . . taking place in our nation and around the world."[30] Unlike contemporary writers, however, King does not isolate references to sight and seeing from a discussion of the body generally and the senses in particular. "I never did intend to adjust myself to the madness of militarism and the self-defeating effects of physical violence," writes

---

[27] Martin Luther King, Jr., "Pilgrimage to Nonviolence," in James M. Washington, ed., *A Testament of Hope, The Essential Writings of Martin Luther King, Jr.* (San Francisco, Harper and Row, 1986), 37-38.

[28] *Ibid.*, 37.

[29] *Ibid.*, 38. The metaphor most widely associated with King develops the Social Christian claim that individuals could employ the vocabulary of personality and personal characteristics to influence and change public life. When King utters the famous refrain "I have a dream," he helps his audience imagine a situation in which an action unique to the self, namely, dreaming, becomes a means of redefining and reforming the social order.

King. To avoid both of these threats to the body, Americans must hear the words of a prophet like Amos, whose voice "echoes across the centuries." They must touch "hands and sing . . . the old Negro spiritual" and feel "justice run like waters and righteousness like a mighty stream." "God is interested . . . in the creation of a society," King maintains, "where every man will respect the dignity and the worth of human personality."[31] Therefore, he calls upon his audience "to see" this nation with "the vision" of Abraham Lincoln; to "look into the eyes of . . . men and women" as did "Jesus of Nazareth."[32]

King's metaphors suggest to his audience that, when they consider the senses together as constitutive elements of an integrated personality, the foundations for broader social reform are laid. Sounding like an earlier social Christian critic of race relations, Amory Bradford, King emphasizes the tension that results when individual "personalities" conflict with their social counterparts. Like Bradford, King does not diminish the role of such tension; in fact, both writers celebrate and expand it: "So let us be maladjusted," asserts King, "for through such maladjustment . . . we will be able to emerge from the bleak and desolate midnight of man's inhumanity to man."[33]

Fifty years before King's "American Dream," Bradford had used similar language to describe the way individuals encounter social elements that "God has united in a single personality." "History needs to be read from the point of view of its interior forces," he wrote, even though that point of view may "arouse new forms of friction."[34] According to Bradford, such friction influences "the body. . . the mind, and . . . the spirit" and stimulates in some "an intellectual and spiritual vision."[35] Bradford's phrase, which indeed joins body, mind, and spirit, enhances

[30] Martin Luther King, Jr., "The American Dream," in Washington, ed., *A Testament of Hope*, 215.

[31] *Ibid.*

[32] *Ibid.*, 216.

[33] *Ibid.*

[34] Amory H. Bradford, *My Brother* (New York: Pilgrim Press, 1910), 247, 255.

[35] *Ibid.*, 16, 246.

the rhetoric of visual experience. Those who reform the social "personality" do so because they recognize alternative ways to lasting brotherhood. Bradford was very specific in the vocabulary he selected to distinguish genuine reformers from those who merely comply with the social order. The latter are "always blind" and refuse "to see that men are made of one blood." By contrast, the former, he wrote, see "the outlines of the picture" and strive to complete the shape.[36]

During the late nineteenth and early twentieth centuries, social Christians imagined such a "public" shape in terms borrowed directly from the realm of "personal" experience. One of the experiences they referred to often and used critically was the act of "dreaming." From Rauschenbusch's lament in *Christianity and the Social Crisis* that "setting up a Christian social order" seemed like "a fair and futile dream," to the dream of death that motivates Sheldon's protagonist in *Robert Hardy's Seven Days*; from Reverend Daikin Burrom's dream of travel between various civilizations in Kay Baily Leach's novel *Souless Saint: A Strange Revelation*, to David Morgan's tale *A Dream of Christ's Return*, these examples—down to and of course including Martin Luther King Jr.'s famous 1963 testament, "I Have a Dream"—have helped social Christians fashion social commentaries that are based on references to the deepest recesses of the human personality.[37]

In a very popular series of novels published between 1869 and 1887, Elizabeth Stuart Phelps Ward imagined ways that heaven and earth interact as certain characters dream about death.[38] The second novel in her series, *Beyond the Gates*, dramatizes this interaction through a lengthy dream sequence. The

---

[36] *Ibid.*, 246-47.

[37] Charles Sheldon, *Robert Hardy's Seven Days; a Dream and Its Consequences* (New York: Street and Smith, 1899); Kay Bailey Leach, *Soulless Saints, A Strange Revelation* (Chicago: American Press, 1983); David Morgan, *A Dream of Christ's Return* (Chicago: Curtis and Jennings, 1899).

[38] Ward, Elizabeth Stuart Phelps, *The Gates Ajar* (Boston: Fields, Osgood, 1869), *Beyond the Gates* (Boston: Houghton Mifflin, 1883), *The Gates Between* (Boston: Houghton Mifflin, 1887).

protagonist, "Miss Mary," a social activist in a Massachusetts "factory town" where she teaches, serves upon the Sanitary Commission, helps at the women's prison, and works "a little" for the State Bureau of Labor, suddenly catches a fever and is confined to bed. Two weeks later she appears to be ready for her journey to heaven where she will join her deceased father. During the next fourteen chapters Mary narrates that journey.

For Mary, the most remarkable discovery is that heaven bears such a close resemblance to earth. Specifically, it resembles earthly realms most familiar to her because she is a woman. "I found myself still involved in certain filial and domestic responsibilities, in intellectual acquisition, in the moral support of others, and in spiritual self-culture."[39] "Just as it is on earth," the "home," according to Mary, is in Heaven "the center of all growth and blessedness."[40] Heavenly marriages are perfect in their "eternal permanency," but life outside of them offers women in heaven nothing more than the familiar set of opportunities.[41] In Mary's case, she is allowed to meet the Civil War soldiers who had been her patients when she served the Union Army as a nurse. When the heavenly society does not treat a woman as "royal," it is because she performs duties that are similar to those that might be expected of her on earth": "philanthropy," the "parlor lecture," and "sustained self-denial."[42]

Rather than challenge this arrangement, Phelps Ward celebrates it. Just as Social Gospel literature tends to allow personal experience to define the social order, in *Beyond the Gates* the qualities and characteristics of temporal existence actually define eternal life. In both instances readers find that social Christian writers use the "part" to provide a vocabulary for understanding the "whole." Phelps Ward does not imagine a heavenly realm that is radically different from its earthly counterpart; instead, she encourages readers to identify in their physical

[39] Phelps Ward, *Beyond the Gates*, 134.
[40] *Ibid.*, 128.
[41] *Ibid.*, 129.

existence some means of reform that will correct social problems and thereby bring the human community closer to its most advanced expression imaginable, the "heavenly city."[43]

In a heavenly realm where social Christians again describe God as a "personality," it follows that Miss Mary experiences the divine through her "senses."[44] "So far from there being any diminution in the number or power of the senses in the spiritual life," she claims, "I found not only an acuter intensity in those which we already possessed, but that the effect of our new conditions was to create others of whose character we had never dreamed." References to the sacred and the profane mix in clumsy but surprising ways as Miss Mary tries to articulate how "celestial life develops the soul of a thing." "When I speak of eating and drinking, for instance, I do not mean that we cooked and prepared our food as we do below. . . . I do mean," she goes on to say, "that the *soul of a sense* is a more exquisite thing than what we may call the body of the sense. . . ."[45]

Although the "soul" of each sense is "exquisite" and should not be isolated, Miss Mary nevertheless claims a unique position for vision among "the varieties of rank in the celestial kingdom."[46] The ability to see "empowers" other senses, and although it leaves the spectator "with no verb or adjective to express" beauty and truth, it nevertheless prepares them to act. "I was ready for any duty," Miss Mary asserts after watching a heavenly symphony of color. "I was strong for all deprivation."[47]

Such a claim again challenges recent critics of this period who read complicity and impotence into its rhetoric of visual experience. Although students of American culture can no longer privilege the religious terminology of

[42] *Ibid.*, 144.
[43] *Ibid.*, 135.
[44] *Ibid.*, 168.
[45] *Ibid.*, 150-51.
[46] *Ibid.*, 140.
[47] *Ibid.*, 166.

a particular era and organize all literary and artistic expressions accordingly, neither can they ignore religious discourse altogether. June Howard may be correct that literary naturalism is the most distinctive cultural form to emerge in the United States during the late nineteenth and early twentieth centuries. She may also be right when she asserts that in one novel, Frank Norris's *The Octopus*, readers "can clearly trace the dynamic that constitutes the form's imminent ideology."[48] However, students of the period cannot ignore the religious dimensions of that ideology in favor of those aspects that emphasize Howard's more Marxist approach. Certain facts remain relevant: in *The Octopus* religious cycles of death and rebirth structure plot; spiritual qualities shape and distinguish characters throughout the novel; the protagonist refers at key moments in the narrative to Saint Paul; various social entities such as the Pacific and Southwestern Railroad—the "octopus" of the title—assume certain "personal" traits that allow readers to distinguish it by their own "sixth" sense.[49]

---

[48] Howard, *Form and History in American Literary Naturalism*, 117.

[49] In addition to such evidence, readers need to consider that one of the most respected social Christian ministers in nineteenth-century New York, W. S. Rainsford, was a close friend of Norris. Rainsford even wrote a brief tribute to Norris for *World's Work* on the occasion of the novelist's untimely death. It is surely no accident that in his tribute Rainsford praised Norris for his ability to cultivate the one physical sense that defined both naturalism and the social Christian movement: "sight." "We need men today who can see," Rainsford wrote, and "seeing things and men as they are . . . can put down accurately what they see." As though he recognized that Naturalism and social Christianity shared a common "personality," Rainsford called on those who appreciated the aims of both movements to "see sanely" as they recorded their observations. For Rainsford, sanity implied belief: to see life "sanely" was to "see it whole," and behind this reference to unity was a motive "to serve" others in need.

Because the motive is explicitly religious, the notion of "service" helps to redefine relationships between self and other, viewer and spectacle. To serve others need not imply that one objectifies them; it also can mean that the server and the one being served relate to one another in ways that engender mutual respect, even love. This is a far cry from the rigid distinctions made by Howard between an impotent bourgeoisie and the "spectacle" of a proletariat "other" in *The Octopus*, and it challenges those approaches to cultural history that tend to substitute a contemporary critical vocabulary for the terms that frame discussions during a particular period. For more complete discussion see John Waldmeir, *The American Trilogy, 1900-1937: Norris, Dreiser, Dos Passos and the History of Mammon* (West Cornwall, CT: Locust Hill Press, 1995).

When readers acknowledge the role of religious discourse in texts and other cultural artifacts from the late nineteenth and early twentieth centuries, they identify specific and in some cases new contexts for those works. Across a wide spectrum of writings best described as "social Christian," for example, readers discover various attempts to describe the "body" in coherent, integrated ways. Metaphors associated with acts of "seeing" correspond to others that refer to touch, taste, hearing, etc. and together they advance a concept of "personality" that Americans from the period ascribe to both individuals and organizations. Subject to the paradigm of creation, fall, and redemption that controls virtually all expressions of "the person" in this culture, the relationship between selves and society becomes both reciprocal and critical. Although we may watch the "spectacle," we are not powerless to criticize it.

CONCLUSION

A NEW SACREDNESS

> The immanence of Christ, the vital unity of the race, the presence of the kingdom—these truths give to life a new sacredness and to duty new cogency.
>
> Washington Gladden

It is not fashionable to find in social Christian discourse from the late nineteenth and early twentieth centuries evidence of a critical idiom. Recent works that examine not only social Christianity from this period but also American culture generally insist that readers cannot construct critical arguments about the culture using terms borrowed from it. Readers must develop their critical perspectives from positions that are decidedly outside the object they study. Today such positions result in primarily three types of questions about a culture and its artifacts: questions related to gender, those concerned with race, and others that deal in matters of economic class.

For example, if one considers Gladden's three "ideas" in the above quotation separately, it becomes clear that they each provide topics for book-length studies. Indeed, those who are interested in the social Christian movement can read the outstanding work of William Hutchison on theological immanence and of Robert Handy or, more recently, Paul T. Phillips, on the Kingdom of God.[1] However, in an era when revisionist historians are re-reading late nineteenth and early twentieth-century "texts" for what they tell us about cultural attitudes toward gender, race, and class, these approaches seem almost anachronistic. If an earlier generation of scholars fastened on terms such as "immanence of Christ" and "presence of the Kingdom" as they appeared in writers like Gladden, current scholars have paid more attention to phrases like "vital unity of the race." In doing so they have produced some fine work.[2] Susan Curtis, for instance, has been able to demonstrate that social Christianity has a very difficult time escaping the influence of economic change during this period. In the late nineteenth and early twentieth centuries a revolution in business management occurred, corporate capitalism emerged, and the nation developed what many critics have called a "culture of consumption." Within such an economic system and its corresponding cultural order, all things became commodities for citizens to "consume." Using terminology from this perspective, Curtis is able to show that "the very act of consuming—that is, participating in and becoming part of a consumer culture—became an act of faith, faith in the messages of corporate and scientific experts and in the ability of commodities and therapeutic professionals to advance a general process of social identification and self-realization." Social Christians were no exception to this process for, as Curtis points out, "the enthusiastic corps" who "spread the social gospel subordinated their faith and practice to secular

---

[1] William Hutchison, *The Modernist Impulse in American Protestantism* (New York: Oxford U. Press, 1976); Robert T. Handy, ed., *The Social Gospel in America* (New York: Oxford U. Press, 1966); Paul T. Phillips, *A Kingdom on Earth, Anglo-American Social Christianity, 1880-1940* (University Park, PA: Pennsylvania State U. Press, 1996).

[2] Two examples are Ralph E. Luker, *The Social Gospel in Black and White, American Racial Reform, 1885-1912* (Chapel Hill: U. of North Carolina Press, 1991); Susan Curtis, *A Consuming Faith: The Social Gospel and Modern American Culture* (Baltimore: The Johns Hopkins U. Press, 1991).

culture," and in this way "the emerging culture of consumption began to define the meaning of the social gospel and to make it a commodity."[3]

Such "commodificaton" may have taken place, but the process does not necessarily leave social Christianity without its own critical voice on this issue. As Giles Gunn points out, if a culture like nineteenth or twentieth-century America cannot think "against" itself, it nevertheless can generate a vocabulary that allows people to think "across" it.

> To think across a culture rather than against it is to suppose that even if we can think in no other terms but those that culture itself provides, we do not have to accept the valuations that culture currently places on them. Our margin of freedom, in this case, derives from two oft-noted but frequently disputed facts. The first is that cultures almost always offer us more than one set of terms in which to do our thinking, which is another way of saying that cultures, however dominant, are never completely hegemonic. The second is that the terms culture provides for thought are rarely if ever perfectly consistent with themselves; discrepancy, disparity, asymmetry, rupture, even contradiction, as post structuralism has taught us, are inevitable.[4]

From the need to reach "wholeness" through images of fragmentation to the quest for "presence" through the rhetoric of "absence"; from the tendency to interpret new lands according to ancient paradigms to the quest for a single plot through the proliferation of competing texts: social Christianity never speaks with one voice. Discrepancy, disparity, asymmetry, rupture and contradiction characterize the rhetoric of this movement in ways that scholars are just beginning to appreciate and note. William McGuire King speculates that "perhaps the original . . . movement, rather than being a monolithic entity, was really an

---

[3] Curtis, *A Consuming Faith*, 229, 238.

[4] Giles Gunn, *Thinking Across the American Grain: Ideology, Intellect, and the New Pragmatism* (Chicago: U. of Chicago Press, 1992), 1. Seven years after Curtis published *A Consuming Faith* she sounded a note of caution similar to Gunn's, pointing out that it is "somewhat troubling" to "try to speak for 'national cultural' trends or argue for the 'dominance' of . . . [certain] terms in the national discourse." Susan Curtis, "The Social Gospel and Race in American Culture" in Christopher H. Evans, ed., *Perspectives on the Social Gospel, Papers from the Inaugural Social Gospel Conference at Colgate Rochester Divinity School* (Lewiston: Edwin Mellen Press, 1999), 16.

alliance or coalition of Christian reformers. . . ."[5] Christopher Evans echoes King's thoughts when he writes that:

> Future generations of scholars will, no doubt, always be indebted to individuals like Charles Hopkins for enabling us to see clearly a scholarly target called "the social gospel." At the same time . . . the target is often an entity dependent upon the questions we ask – or fail to ask. As we are able to keep raising new questions, we may acknowledge that good scholarship is not always about hitting the bull's eye.[6]

If the historian Ralph Luker is correct when he claims that, prior to the organization of the Federal Council of Churches in 1908 "there is little evidence of interaction among the social gospel's leading advocates or its local centers," then it probably is true that no bull's eye exists and that students of the movement will never "define" a single Social Gospel or categorize all elements of an even larger social Christianity.[7]

In the end, however, that may be the point. In his pioneering study of the Social Gospel, C. Howard Hopkins uses the above quote from Washington Gladden to undertake a chapter titled "Evolution and the Kingdom." Hopkins claims that the passage provides readers with "three clearly related ideas that together constituted a logical and unified frame of reference for social Christianity. These were," he explains, "the immanence of God, the organic or solidaristic view of society, and the presence of the kingdom of heaven on earth."[8] The assertion has controlled more than a generation of studies dedicated to the social Christian movement. In broad surveys of social Christianity as well as studies focused exclusively on the Social Gospel, critics have accepted the basic

---

[5] William McGuire King, "The Emergence of Social Gospel Radicalism: The Methodist Case," Church History 50 (1981): 437.

[6] Christopher H. Evans, "Defining the Target: Perspectives on the Social Gospel" in Evans, *Perspectives on the Social Gospel*, xxii.

[7] Ralph E. Luker, "Interpreting the Social Gospel: Reflections on To Generations of Historiography," in *Ibid.*, 6.

[8] C. Howard Hopkins, *The Rise of the Social Gospel in American Protestantism*, 1865-1915 (New Haven: Yale U. Press, 1940), 123.

structure implied by Hopkins' frame of reference. They have had good reasons; generally, it is correct.

However, although these three ideas constitute an accurate context for social Christian research and scholarship, they do not necessarily correlate very well. In fact, their discrepancies are many, significant and, in the end, necessary to the movement. Social Christianity has endured in large part because its key ideas have not been restricted by a rigid discourse that appeals only to a narrow audience. Recall that God's "immanence" and "Kingdom," for example, mean something quite different to the "race" as it moves away from urban centers in the east to the mountains and plains west of the Mississippi. Some would extend that reach even father. Jesuit scholar Roger Haight, for example, argues that social Christianity, especially the late nineteenth and early twentieth-century Social Gospel, is diverse enough to cross denominational, cultural, even temporal borders. He compares the movement to contemporary theologies of liberation, especially as articulated by Latin American bishops and Roman Catholic theologians. For Haight, both social Christianity and liberation theology offer believers the chance to "take up a perspective of solidarity with all others and interpret Christian doctrine accordingly."[9]

"Once this perspective is opened," writes Haight, "the whole world becomes the horizon of the imagination." Late nineteenth and early twentieth-century social Christians looked toward a horizon that promised God's immanence, social solidarity, and a divine kingdom on earth. They frequently held the ideas together and made them present through a form of prose that was both imaginative and critical. When they did, their ideas led them to the "truths" Gladden speaks of in the second half of the above quotation. The interactions of "immanence," "racial unity," and "the Kingdom of God" resulted in changes to the ways ministers, theologians, novelists, social scientists, poets, painters and others represented "the sacred" and performed some "duty" toward it.

---

[9] Roger Haight, "Liberation Theology and the Social Gospel," *Grail* 5 (1989): 55

In 1889 the pastor who first used the term "social Gospel," C.O. Brown, helped his Dubuque, Iowa congregation celebrate their semi-centennial. For several days parish members heard a number of ministers describe national changes as evidence of a new "horizon" for individuals and society. This particular metaphor of a changing "horizon" appears in divers homilies and speeches from the festivities, although its meaning varies considerably. For the Reverend J.C. Holbrook, the horizon represents that moment when, steeped in faith, the human imagination is able to transform the lives of individuals and nations. To "the eye of faith," writes Holbrook, "the horizon is all aglow with indications" that "the morning cometh" when "the Sun of Righteousness shall rise upon the nations with healing in his wings and dissipate the darkness which has long overshadowed so many lands and fill the earth with the splendor of his full orbed glory."[10] For the Rev. C.E. Harrington the metaphor suggests theological reforms through an attitude that inspires "reverence for the past" but also "courage to set . . . [one's] face towards the east and look for the day-dawn and the sunlight of truth."[11] For C.O. Brown the horizon describes a place of "progress," like the American "frontier . . . no longer bounded by Indian camps and scenes of blood, but only by the commerce-bearing seas."[12]

One could organize these interpretations of the "horizon" metaphor in various ways (though it is interesting to recognize the extent to which Holbrook's reference suggests a discussion of God's Kingdom, Harrington's implies the Lord's immanence, and Brown's introduces the issue of race—albeit in a disappointing and ugly way). In the end, however, what matters is not simply that readers can distinguish between these interpretations using terminology borrowed from Gladden's quotation but that all three uses coexist easily in Brown's book;

[10] J.C. Holbrook, "The Sign of the Times" in C.O. Brown, ed., *Semi-Centennial Celebration of the First Congregational Church of Dubuque, Iowa* (Dubuque: First Congregational Church, 1889), 11.

[11] C.E. Harrington, "The Heroic Age of Congregationalism," in Brown, *Semi-Centennial Celebration*, 51.

[12] C.O. Brown, "Address of Welcome," in *Ibid.*, 7.

the audience at the First Congregational Church in Dubuque never saw any reason to separate them. If scholars today isolate them it should be to understand or at least acknowledge that, because they acquire meaning from one another, they belong together.

Such an approach demands that across all aspects of social Christian thought and practice we cast a wide net. Late nineteenth and early twentieth-century social Christians met the sacred at the crossroads of individual and social redemption and imagined life in its presence. But those roads did not intersect in only one place, nor did they motivate a uniform response. One answer, therefore, to Ralph Luker's question—"In what meaningful sense can the 'social gospel movement' be understood as a 'social movement' at all?"—would be that all "movement" associated with the phrase depends primarily upon acts of imagination. In the imagined characters and landscapes of novels, paintings, and poetry, social Christians motivated one another to interact in ways that kept the movement a diffuse, ecumenical entity. When today we search for "the center" in those theological ideas that have helped social Christianity endure, we cannot avoid the traces of figurative expression that enliven its rhetoric and sustain its prose. "Read the history of doctrine," argues Washington Gladden in his sermon "Society Building," "and you will find how one generation after another has sent its theological doctrines to the junkpile and the ash heap." Although Gladden's words provide no apparent answer to Luker's question, they do invite readers to imagine a social Christianity on the move: away from the "ash heap" and toward what advocates from Sheldon to Woods, Tourgee to Rauschenbusch, Gladden to Martin Luther King Jr. have realized: that, in theological systems, "Finality is no more possible . . . than . . . a final statement of the number and size and form of the branches and leaves on a growing tree."[13] "Light up The Word," writes

[13] Washington Gladden, sermon, "Society Building," April 9, 1883. Quoted in C. George Fry, "The Social Gospel at the Crossroads of Middle America: Washington Solomon Gladden and the First Congregational Church, Columbus, Ohio, 1882-1918," in Evans, *Perspectives on the Social Gospel*, 61-62.

Gladden in the lyrics to his hymn, "O Lord of Life," "the fettered page from killing bondage free." Such is the prayer of those who would release the imagination to articulate a more cogent sense of social Christian duty.

SOURCES

Abbott, Lyman. *Christianity and Social Problems*. Boston: Houghton Mifflin, 1896.

Abell, Aaron. *The Urban Impact on American Protestantism, 1865-1900.* Cambridge: Harvard U. Press, 1943.

Barton, C. Josephine. *Evangel Ahvallah: or, The White Spectrum*. Kansas City: the Author, 1895.

Bates, Katherine Lee. "The Ideal." *The Dawn* 2:6 (October, 1890): 229.

Beard, Frank. "Old Time Art and Artists." *Our Day* (February, 1896): 85-91.

Black, George D. "Editorial." *The Kingdom* (February 3, 1898): 323.

Bliss, W.D.P. "Salutamus." *The Dawn* 1:1 (May 15, 1889): 1.

Boase, Paul H. ed. *The Rhetoric of Christian Socialism.* New York: Random House, 1969.

Rachel Bowlby, *Just Looking: Consumer Culture in Dreiser, Gissing, and Zola*. New York: Methuen, 1985.

Boyer, Paul S. "*In His Steps*: A Reappraisal." *American Quarterly* 23 (Spring 1971): 60-78.

Bradford, Amory H. *My Brother*. New York: Pilgrim Press, 1910.

Brewer, David J, ed.. *The World's Best Orations*. Volume 2. St. Louis: Fred P. Kaiser, 1900.

Brown, C.O. ed., *Semi Centennial Celebration of the First Congregational Church of Dubuque, Iowa, May 12th and 13th, 1889*. Dubuque: First Congregational Church, 1889.

________. *Talks on the Labor Troubles*. Chicago: F.H. Revel, 1886.

Buford, Thomas O. "Personalism and Education: A Philosophical Retrospect/Prospect." *Proceedings of the Twentieth World Congress of Philosophy* (1998). *The Paideia Project* at www.bu.edu/wcp/Papers/Educ/EducBufo.

Cawelti, John. "Changing Ides of Social Reform as Seen in Selected American Novels of the 1850s, the 1880s, and the Present Day." *Social Service Review* 35 (1961): 278-289.

Chase, Thomas. *The English Religious Lexis*. Lewiston: Edwin Mellen Press, 1988.

Clarke, William Newton. *Sixty Years with the Bible, A Record of Experience.* New York: Charles Scribner's Sons, 1912.

Crawford, T.C. *A Man and His Soul, An Occult Romance of Washington Life.* New York: Charles B. Reed, 1894.

Curtis, Susan. *A Consuming Faith, The Social Gospel and Modern American Culture.* Baltimore: Johns Hopkins U. Press, 1991.

Davies, Wallace Evans. "Religious Issues in Late Nineteenth-Century American Novels. *Bulletin of the John Rylands Library* 41 (1959): 328-59.

Dorn, Jacob. "The Social Gospel and Socialism: A Comparison of the Thought of Francis Greenwood Peabody, Washington Gladden, and Walter Rauschenbusch." *Church History* 62 (1993): 82-100.

Dorrien, Gary. "Liberal Socialism and the Legacy of the Social Gospel." *Cross Currents* 39 (1989): 339-354.

Dutton, Clarence. *Tertiary History of the Grand Canyon District*, United States Geological Survey, Director J.W. Powell. Washington: Government Printing Office, 1882.

Ellison, Nine E. *Nadine: Romance of Two Lives*. Nashville: Gospel Advocate Publishing Co., 1897.

Ely, Richard T. *Socialism.* New York, 1894.;

Elzey, Wayne. "What Would Jesus Do?" *In His Steps* and the Moral Codes of the Middle Class. *Soundings* 58 (Winter, 1975): 463-489.

Etulain, Richard. *Re-Imagining the Modern American West, A Century of Fiction, History, and Art.* Tucson: U. of Arizona, 1996.

Evans, Christopher H. *Perspectives on the Social Gospel: Papers from the Inaugural Social Gospel Conference at Colgate Rochester Divinity School.* Lewiston: Edwin Mellen Press, 1999.

Ferre, John P. *A Social Gospel for the Millions, The Religious Bestsellers of Charles Sheldon, Charles Gordon, and Harold Bell Wright.* Bowling Green, OH: Bowling Green State U. Press, 1988.

Fifty Great Cartoons. Chicago, The Ram's Horn Press, 1899.

Fisher, Philip. "Acting, Reading Fortune's Wheel: *Sister Carrie* and the Life History of Objects," *American Literary Realism: New Essays*, Eric J. Sundquist, ed. (Baltimore: Johns Hopkins U. Press): 259-77

Fisher, Philip. "Appearing and Disappearing in Public: Social Space in Late Nineteenth-Century American Culture." In Harvard English Series, *Reconstructing American Literary History*. Sacvan Bercovitch, ed. Cambridge: Harvard U. Press, 1986: 155-88.

Fitch, Charles H. "The Coming of the Dawn." *The Dawn* 1:1 (May 15, 1889): 1.

Gates, George A. "Prospectus for *The Kingdom*." *The Kingdom* (April 20, 1894): 1-3.

Gerdts, William H. *Art Across America: The Plains States and the West*. New York: Abbeville Press, 1990.

Gilman, Nicholas Paine. "Christian Socialism in America." *Unitarian Review* 32 (1889): 350-66.

Gladden, Washington. *The Christian League of Connecticut*. New York: Century, 1883.

________. *The Relations of Art and Morality*. New York: Wilbur B. Ketchum, 1897.

________. *Social Facts and Forces*. New York: G.P. Putnam's Sons, 1897.

________. *Witnesses of the Light*. Freeport: Books for Libraries Press, 1903.

Gorrell, Donald K. *The Age of Social Responsibility, The Social Gospel in the Progressive Era*. Macon: Mercer U. Press, 1988.

Green, Garrett. *Imagining God, Theology and the Religious Imagination*. Grand Rapids: Wm. B. Eerdman's, 1989.

Gunn, Gunn. *Thinking Across the American Grain: Ideology, Intellect, and the New Pragmatism*. Chicago: U. of Chicago Press, 1992.

Edward Everett Hale, *If Jesus Came to Boston*. Boston: Lamson, Wolffe, 1895.

Haight, Roger. "Liberation Theology and the Social Gospel," *Grail* 5 (1989): 45-57.

Hall, Charles Cuthbert. *The Universal Elements of the Christian Religion*. New York: Fleming H. Revell, 1905.

Howard, June. *Form and History in American Literary Naturalism*. Chapel Hill: U. of North Carolina Press, 1985.

Handy, Robert T. *The Social Gospel in America 1870-1920: Gladden, Ely, Rauschenbusch*. New York, Oxford U. Press, 1966.

Herron, George Davis. *The Christian Society.* Chicago Fleming H. Revel Company, 1894.

________. *The Larger Christ.* Chicago: Fleming H. Revel, 1891.

________. "Letter." *The Kingdom* (April, 1894): 4-5.

________. *The New Redemption.* New York: Thomas Y. Crowell, 1893.

Hill, Beveridge. *The Story of a Canon.* Boston: Arena Publishing Co., 1895.

Hopkins, C. Howard and Ronald C. White, eds. *The Social Gospel: Religion and Reform in a Changing America.* Philadelphia: Temple U. Press, 1976.

C. Howard Hopkins, *The Rise of the Social Gospel in American Protestantism, 1865 –1915.* New Haven: Yale U. Press, 1940.

Hudson, Winthrop, ed. *Walter Rauschenbusch, Selected Writings.* New York: Paulist Press, 1984.

Hutchison, William R. "The Americanness of the Social Gospel: An Inquiry in Comparative History. *Church History* 44 (1975): 367-81.

________. *The Modernist Impulse in American Protestantism.* New York: Oxford U. Press, 1976.

Kaplan, Amy. *The Social Construction of American Realism.* Chicago: U. Chicago Press, 1988.

Kennedy, J.Gerald. *Imagining Paris: Exile, Writing, and American Identity.* New Haven: Yale U. Press, 1993.

King, Henry Churchill. *Theology and the Social Consciousness.* New York: Macmillan, 1907.

King, William McGuire. "The Emergence of Social Gospel Radicalism: The Methodist Case," *Church History* 50 (1981): 436-449.

________. "'History as Revelation' in the Theology of the Social Gospel," *Harvard Theological Review* 76 (1983): 109-129

Kort, Wesley A. *Bound to Differ, The Dynamics of Theological Discourses.* University Park: Pennsylvania State U. Press, 1992.

Leach, Kay Bailey. *Soulless Saints, A Strange Revelation.* Chicago: American Press, 1983.

Lindley, Susan H. "Women and the Social Gospel Novel." *American Society of Church History* 54 (1985): 56-73.

Long, Lisa A. "'The Corporality of Heaven': Rehabilitating the Civil War Body in The Gates Ajar." *American Literature* 69 (1997) 781-811.

Luker, Ralph E. *The Social Gospel in Black and White: American Racial Reform, 1885-1912*. Chapel Hill: U. of North Carolina Press, 1991.

Lyman, Eugene. *The God of the New Age*. Boston: Pilgrim, 1918.

MacArthur, James. "A Christian Socialist in Fiction." *The Dawn* 3:10 (January 1892): 3-4

May, Henry F. *Protestant Churches and Industrial America.* New York: Octagon Books, 1949, 1977.

Martin, Ronald E. *American Literature and the Universe of Force*. Durham: Duke U. Press, 1981.

Marty, Martin E. *Modern American Religion*, vol. 1, *The Irony of It All, 1893-1919*. Chicago: U. of Chicago Press, 1986.

Mays, Benjamin E. ed., *A Gospel for the Social Awakening, Selections from the Writings of Walter Rauschenbusch*. New York: Association Press, 1950.

________. *The Negro's God as Reflected in His Literature*. New York: Russell and Russell, 1938.

McCowan, Archibald. *Christ, the Socialist.* Boston: Arena Publishing, 1894.

McKay, Charles. "Clear the Way." *The Dawn* 1:2 (June, 1889): 1.

Morgan, David. *A Dream of Christ's Return*. Chicago: Curtis and Jennings, 1899.

Nicholl, Grier. "The Christian Novel and Social Gospel Evangelism." *Religion in Life* 34 (1965): 548-61).

Norris, Kathleen. *The Cloister Walk.* New York: Routledge: 1996.

North Dakota Magazine 1 (1906).

Nye, Russel B. *Midwestern Progressive Politics, A Historical Study of Its Origins and Development, 1870-1950*. East Lansing: Michigan State College Press,

Phillips, Paul T. *A Kingdom on Earth: Anglo-American Social Christianity, 1880-1940*. University Park, PA.: Pennsylvania State U. Press.

Pizer, Donald. *American Thought and Writing: The 1890s*. Boston: Houghton Mifflin, 1972.

Pounds, Jesse H.. *The Ironclad Pledge: A Story of Christian Endeavor*. Cincinnati: Standard Publishing Co., 1894.

Quantic, Diane Dufva. *The Nature of the Place, A Study of Great Plains Fiction*. Lincoln: U. of Nebraska Press, 1995.

Rauschenbusch, Walter. *Christianity and the Social Crisis*. Ed. Robert D. Cross. New York: Harper Torchbooks, 1964.

________. *Christianizing the Social Order*. New York: Macmillan, 1913.

________. *A Theology for the Social Gospel*. New York: Macmillan Co., 1917.

Reed, Isaac George. *From Heaven to New York*. New York: Optimus Printing Co., 1894; first published 1875.

Roohan, James E. "American Catholics and the Social Question, 1865-1900." United States Catholic Historical Society *Historical Records and Studies* 43 (1955): 3-26.

Schlesinger, Arthur, M. A Ciritcal Period in American Religion, 1875-1900." Massachusetts Historical Society *Proceedings* 64 (1932): 522-548.

Sheldon, Charles. *Charles M. Sheldon, His Life Story*. New York: George H. Doran, 1925.

________. *The Crucifixion of Phillip Strong*. Chicago: A.C. McClurg and Co., 1894.

________. *The First Christian Daily Paper and Other Sketches*. New York: Street and Smith, 1899.

________. *In His Steps* (New York: Books, Inc., nd.), 243.

________. *The Miracle at Markham*. Chicago: John H. Ulrich, 1899.

________. "A Newspaperman for a Week," in *The First Christian Daily Paper*.

________. *The Redemption of Freetown*. Boston: United Society of Christian Endeavor, 1898.

________. *Richard Bruce or The Life That Now Is*. Chicago: Advance Publishing, 1898.

Sheldon, Charles. *Robert Hardy's Seven Days; a Dream and Its Consequences*. New York: Street and Smith, 1899.

Smith, Gary Scott. "Charles M. Sheldon's *In His Steps* in the Context of Religion and Culture in Late Nineteenth-Century America." *Fides et Historia* 22 (1990): 47-69.

________. "When Stead Came to Chicago: The `Social Gospel Novel' and the Chicago Civic Federation." *American Presbyterians* 68 (1990): 193-205.

Stead, William T. *If Christ Came to Chicago*. Chicago: Laird and Lee, 1894.

Strong, Josiah. *Our Country*. Ed. Jurgen Herbst. Cambridge: Harvard U. Press, 1963.

Suderman, Elmer F. "Criticisms of the Protestant Church in the American Novel: 1870-1900. *Midcontinent American Studies Journal* 5 (1964): 17-23.

________. "Religion in the Popular American Novel: 1870-1900. *Journal of Popular Culture* 9 (1976): 1003-1009.

________. "The Social-Gospel Novelists' Criticism of American Society." *Midcontinent American Studies Journal* 7 (1966): 45-60.

Thomas, George M. *Revivalism and Cultural Change, Christianity, Nation Building, and the Market in the Nineteenth-Century United States*. Chicago: U. of Chicago Press, 1989.

Tourgee, Albion. *Murvale Eastman, Christian Socialist*. New York: Fords, Howard, & Hulbert, 1889.

Ward, Elizabeth Stuart Phelps. *Beyond the Gates* (Boston: Houghton Mifflin, 1883.

________. *The Gates Ajar*. Boston: Fields, Osgood, 1869.

________. *The Gates Between*. Boston: Houghton Mifflin, 1887.

Washington, James M. *A Testament of Hope, The Essential Writings of Martin Luther King, Jr.* San Francisco, Harper and Row, 1986.

Waldmeir, John. *The American Trilogy, 1900-1937: Norris, Dreiser, Dos Passos and the History of Mammon*. West Cornwall, CT: Locust Hill Press, 1995.

White, Ronald C. *Liberty and Justice for All: Racial Reform and the Social Gospel (1877-1925)*. San Francisco: Harper and Row, 1990

Wilkison, Hazel. "Social Thought in American Fiction." *Studies in Sociology* 3 (1918): 1-17.

Wolcott, Julia Anna. "Two Prayers." *The Dawn* 2:7 (November 1890): 301.

Woods, Katherine Pearson. *Metzerott, Shoemaker*. New York: Thomas Y. Crowell, 1889.

Wright, Robert Glenn. *The Social Christian Novel.* Westport, CT: Greenwood Press, 1989.

INDEX

MAGAZINES
Century 31
North America Review 83
North Dakota Magazine 70
The Christian Century 6
The Dawn 3, 21, 23, 87
The Kingdom 3, 85
The Ram's Horn 13, 14, 23, 47
World's Work 111

PRIMARY SOURCES
Abbott, Lyman 97
Christianity and Social Problems 11, 13
"Christinaity versus Socialism" 83-85, 98
Adams, Frederick, Upham 77
Arnold, Matthew
Bates, Katherine Lee 22
Beard, Frank 13-15, 24, 32
Bellamy, Edward 20, 23, 77
Bingham, J.S. 12, 13
Black, George D. 85
Bliss, William Dwight Porter 21, 78, 87, 98
Bradford, Amory 107-108
Brown, Charles O. 10, 11, 12, 118-119
Bryan, William Jennings 73-74
Clarke, William Newton 1, 3, 4
Conwell, Russell 78
Cook, Joseph 78,97
Crawford, T.C. 24-25, 32-34
Crosby, Ernest H. 77
Dafoe, Daniel 11
Debs, Eugene 77
Dutton, Clarence 61
Ellison, Nina 58, 63, 71, 76
Ely, Richard T. 62, 78
Fitch, Charles H. 21-22
Flower, B.O. 77
Garland, Hamlin 77
Gates, George 85, 97, 101-103
George, Henry 77
Progress and Poverty 10
Gilman, N. Paine 78
Gladden, Washington 3, 5, 20, 34, 62, 77, 113
The Christian League of Connecticut 29-31, 32
"The Incarnation" 27
"Migrations and Their Lessons" 53
The Relations of Art and Morality 31
Social Facts and Forces 53
"Society Building" 119
Witnesses of the Light 31
Gordon, Charles 2,
Hale, Edward Everett 42
Hall, Charles Cuthbert 99
Harrington, C.E. 118
Hawthorne, Nathaniel 13
Herron George D. 78, 79
The Christian Society 86
The Larger Christ 86
The New Redemption 86
"The Political Economy of the Lord's Prayer" 80-84, 86, 93
Hill, Berveridge 65, 74
Howells, William Dean 77
Jefferson, Thomas 77
King, Henry Churchill 15
Leach, Kay Baily 108
Lyman, Eugene 15
MacArthur, James 23, 87
McCowan, Archibald 93
Milton, John 11
Morgan, David 108
Norris, Frank 111-112
Pingree, Hazen 77
Pounds, Jessie 58-59, 65
Rainsford, W.S. 111
Rauschenbusch, Walter 3, 5, 20, 23
Christianity and the Social Crisis 55-56, 69, 104, 108
Christianizing the Social Order 104
The New Evangelism 104
Prayers of the Social Awakening 104
"The Social Meaning of the Lord's Prayer" 80-84
The Social Principles of Jesus 104
Theology of the Social Gospel 98, 100, 104
Unto Me 104
Reed, Isaac George 101
Roosevelt, Theodore 61

Savage, Minot 78
Sheldon, Charles 2, 77
 Charles M. Sheldon, His Life Story 50-51
 The Crucifixion of Phillip Strong 35, 43, 51
 In His Steps 34, 35, 37, 39, 43, 44, 45 46 49, 101
 "Law of Christian Discipleship" 37
 Malcolm Kirk 42
 Miracle at Markham 36, 37, 38
 "Newspaperman for a Week" 48
 Redemption of Freetown 36, 37, 49-50
 Richard Bruce 58, 65
 Robert Hardy's Seven Days 108
Simpson, Jerry 77
Stead, Wiiliam T. 101
Strong, Josish 8, 16, 20, 55-56, 59-61
Tolstoy, Leo 77
Tourgee, Albion 88-93
Turner, Frederisck Jackson 60
Ward, Elizabeth Stuart Phelps 108-110
Whittier, John Greenleaf 13, 27
Willard, Francis 86
Wilson, Woodrow 72
Wolcott, Julia Anna 22
Woods, Katherine Pearson 23, 87-88
Wright, Harold Bell 2

SECONDARY SOURCES
Benjamin E. Mays 104-105
Boase, Paul H. 6
Bowlby, Rachel 103
Boyer, Paul 39
Chase, Thomas 9
Curtis, Susan 79, 114, 115
Elzey, Wayne 36, 38
Etulain, Richard 69
Evans, Christopher 116, 119
Ferre, John P. 2
Fisher, Philip 102-103
Fry, George 119
Gorrell, Donald 26, 78, 80, 100
Green, Garrett 5
Gunn, Giles 115
Haight, Roger 117
Handy, Robert 27, 62 114
Hobsbawn, Eric 20
Hopkins, C. Howard 6, 8, 9, 10, 78, 116
Howard, June 102-103, 111
Hutchison, William 3, 5 7, 28, 29, 63, 99, 114
Kaplan, Amy 103
Kennedy, J. Gerald 59-60
King, Martin Luther 105-107
King, William McGuire 15, 16, 115
Kort, Wesley 26
Luker, Ralph 98, 99, 105, 114, 116
Martin, Ronald E. 9
Marty, Martin E. 8, 9, 10, 19, 20, 21, 30
May, Henry F. 5, 6, 7, 78
Norris, Kathleen 71
Nye, Russel B. 77-78
Phillips, Paucl T. 78, 79, 114
Quantic, Diane Dufva 59
Schlesinger, Arthur i
Tylor, Mark C. 19
Waldmeir, John 112
White, Ronald 6, 9, 10, 78
Wright, Robert Glenn 2, 5, 6, 7, 102

TOPICS
Character 1, 82, 83, 84, 90, 91, 95, 101
Christian socialism 8, 77, 78, 81, 83, 86, 87
Climax 43, 44
Commodification 115
Gold Standard 74
Holy Bible 34, 52, 77, 87, 99
 Hebrews 55
 Matthew 79, 81-82
 1 Peter 47, 48
Image(s) 16, 75, 91
Immanence 1, 4, 5, 28, 99
Irony 9
Narrator 30, 33, 93
Narrative 44, 64,
Personalism 95, 97-98, 108
Plot(s) 1, 4, 16, 40, 44, 82-86, 90, 91, 94, 95
Progressivism 100
Protagonist 32, 111
Social Gospel 6, 7, 9, 26, 78, 79, 81, 83, 109
Story 1, 5, 32, 94
Style 1, 5, 44, 81
Uncle Tom's Cabin, 11

VISUAL ART
Art 61-76, 94

Eisele, Christian 61

Gausta, Hejörn 71-72
Grafström, Olof 61, 66-68
Harvey, George 61, 65, 66-68, 76
Hitchens, Joseph 61, 66-68
Learned, Harry 61, 66-68
Wallace J. Laurie 73-74

TEXTS AND STUDIES IN THE SOCIAL GOSPEL

1. Christopher H. Evans, **Social Gospel Liberalism and the Ministry of Ernest Fremont Tittle**
2. Walter Rauschenbusch, **The Righteousness of the Kingdom**, edited and introduced by Max L. Stackhouse
3. **Perspectives on the Social Gospel: Papers from the Inaugural Social Gospel Conference at Colgate Rochester Divinity**, edited by Christopher H. Evans
4. John C. Waldmeir, **Poetry, Prose and Art in the American Social Gospel Movement, 1880-1910**